SILHOUETTES: ISSUE OF BLACK & WHITE AMERICA

A Journey through Black History
as told by a White Professor

BY MICHAEL L. WESTON
Associate Professor of History and Political Studies

Order this book online at **www.trafford.com**
or email orders@trafford.com

Most Trafford titles are also available at major online book retailers.

Printed in the United States of America.

ISBN: 978-1-4669-0653-2 (sc)
ISBN: 978-1-4669-0652-5 (hc)
ISBN: 978-1-4669-0654-9 (e)

Library of Congress Control Number: 2011961939

Trafford rev. 12/29/2011

 www.trafford.com

North America & International
toll-free: 1 888 232 4444 (USA & Canada)
phone: 250 383 6864 ♦ fax: 812 355 4082

TABLE OF CONTENTS

INTRODUCTION

IT IS MY intention to take the reader on a journey of historical perspective, racial delineation, and introspective growth. To walk a mile in someone else's shoes is not always sufficient so as to appropriately understand his or her particular point of view. A better appreciation can be had, when those accoutrements are worn over a more extended period of time. For approximately four months I wore those shoes, and while in them, they never did feel quite comfortable. Nonetheless, they did sustain me on the path toward heightened consciousness and understanding. Within the constraints of a college lecture forum, utilizing a cross-section of both African American and Caucasian students, I will attempt through historical foundations, learned experiences and personal observation, to examine the social threads which weave together the mosaic fabric that is American society. At the same time I will examine issues of contemporary racial relevance, which continue to undermine the pillars on which the nation's social foundations rest. In using the city of Buffalo and its greater metropolitan area as both a backdrop and as a microcosm for racial relations in America, I will attempt to expose misconceptions held by both races, black and white. I will further dissect existing divisive elements found within my own classroom and so often deeply entrenched within black and white cultures. Time has the propensity in which to distort one's perspectives when recounting events of the past. Keeping this in mind, I will to the best of my ability accurately reflect upon events as they transpired for me in the momentous spring of 2000.

On a typical dismal and gray January day in suburban Buffalo, New York, I received a telephone call from a department chairperson of our local community college, commonly referred to as Erie Community College or ECC. As an adjunct professor at ECC it was not altogether uncommon that I would receive a last minute request by the Department of History to instruct a specific course. This request, however, was unusual in that the Department Chairperson indicated that this request in particular would require a high degree of sensitivity. She went on to explain that the course in question–History 103 African American History–would probably have a high concentration of African American students. As a Caucasian professor, I immediately understood the ramifications thereof, and the extent of sensitivity that would be required in its successful execution. The implication being that a white professor teaching African American History to a predominately black group of students in an inner city collegiate environment, might indeed prove to be contentious at the very least, if not altogether offensive.

As a former stock car racer, a fireman with over twenty years' experience, and as a teacher who was part of the United Nations' program to teach Polish and Russian students, I was not then, nor am I now, easily intimidated. In retrospect, I probably did not give the matter the ample attention it warranted and, with my customary zeal for opportunity and challenge, I immediately gave the affirmative, even thanking the Department Chairperson (herself an African American) for the "opportunity." Within days I was in receipt of the ascribed text, <u>From Slavery to Freedom: a History of African Americans</u>, authored in part by one of America's premier authorities on the subject, John Hope Franklin. Already having an educational foundation pertaining to this topic, and with an intense curiosity for all matters related, I immediately began to devour the text.

The Buffalo area has a long past in relation to the history and struggle of African Americans. Its geographical location (a shared border with Canada), manufacturing past, and more liberal and progressive views on matters of race, has for most of the post Civil War era placed Buffalo at the forefront of how racial issues have affected history for blacks and white Americans. With a plethora of way stations on the underground railroad (the most famous, the Michigan Street Baptist Church, almost nearly adjacent to the college), Buffalo has hosted such black luminaries as Harriet Tubman, who escorted escaped slaves across the Niagara River into Canada, and W.E.B. Du Bois, who used the Buffalo region as a springboard for his

Niagara Movement, which ultimately became the forerunner to the National Association for the Advancement of Colored People or the N.A.A.C.P. Further illustrative of Buffalo's more liberal perspective and changing demographics can be found in its recently elected black mayor, and in the appointment of its new African American police commissioner, both of whom are well educated and highly innovative. My own family and I have African American friends. My in-laws have helped raise, as a foster family, over fifty children, many of whom have been special needs, or are minorities, and whom my wife and I at times have helped care for. These children have been integrated into family events such as birthdays and holidays. My own children, in light of this exposure, have been raised so as not to distinguish between the two cultures. But admittedly, I reside in the suburban region of Buffalo which tends to be less than cosmopolitan in its racial composition. My children attend schools with few, if any, African American children. Having black acquaintances, hosting black foster children and educating oneself in African American traditions is not the same as living the black experience, a lesson I was about to learn.

Day one of my lectures and a new adventure would begin in similar fashion to all other previous first days. Long hair, mustache, blazer (minus the suede elbow patches), tie, vest and with a leather briefcase, I certainly looked the part, but this opening day would prove, in fact, to be quite different from all the others. As anticipated, the vast majority of students were African American with approximately one third being white, and with one or two Hispanic students As students began to coalesce outside of the lecture hall and adjacent to the door, I immediately noticed several students who peeked in intermittently, giving the most harsh and hostile of glances. Some black students, in an overt display of displeasure, walked into the lecture room, shook their heads in great disdain and anger, and, then, making the most abrupt about face, left the classroom, presumably never to return. Those who remained sat down, (thumping themselves into their seats) and proceeded to segregate themselves accordingly. As I faced the student body, African Americans largely seated to my right with the Caucasian students skewed more to the left. Just as is often done in American society, so too had the students segregated themselves. I was most ill prepared for the hostile reception I was receiving; perhaps even appalled might be a more appropriate description.

As is my style when lecturing, I choose to employ vigor, humor, movement and, in order to facilitate interaction; I most earnestly encourage dialogue between myself and the students. It seemed to me that the infusion of humor into this venue would be most difficult, if not impossible. The tension and blatant hostility I felt was palpable. If I was to be successful in this endeavor, it was clear new strategies would have to be employed. I have always had a reputation among students as being open and frank. I decided to abandon a humorous approach, and opt instead for a more candid historical perspective, even if it meant occasionally offending my own race by giving the most graphic, poignant, and accurate depiction of the history of events between the two races.

I was aided in these efforts by a mature student who bore a striking resemblance, not only in appearance but in demeanor as well, to one of my favorite Hollywood actors, Morgan Freeman., I found great comfort in discussions with this gentleman during and after lectures. Approximately twenty years my senior, this man afforded me great academic respect. In this first class, he set the tone for future lectures when he exclaimed that he was slightly surprised to see a white professor teaching African American history, but he concluded that he wished to remain and see if I knew my material. In other words, given my academic credentials, he was at least willing to give this "white boy" the benefit of the doubt. He had grown up in the South during the 1950's and 60's and by definition was "old school." He had seen the dark side of discrimination. His presence in my lectures was always a source of comfort. In many respects, he was a living microcosm of history itself and, as such, he was often the tempering factor in the sometimes heated classroom discussions that would ultimately follow. Occasionally, after evening lectures, I would give him a ride home to his rather rundown inner-city neighborhood, and I felt guilty at times when returning to my own more affluent neighborhood with its more expensive homes and manicured lawns.

Throughout the transmission of the course, numerous contentious and fluid topics continued to surface in our weekly evening lectures. Admittedly, and at times with great impunity, I would often "stir the pot" so as to promote such dialogue. Among the most volatile of those were issues relating to slavery, emancipation proclamation, poverty, economic exploitation, racial inequality, restitution, racial profiling, affirmative action, welfare, family structure, the race card and matters of geographic segregation. It was not only my position, but also my intent, to convey the information that my education, experiences and background have afforded me, and also to advocate when possible, even at the risk of offending members of my own ethnic background, views relative to both sides on any given issue pertaining to the black experience within the parameters of American history.

I will address topics of a more contemporary nature in the second half of this book on matters of race in America. This follows the pattern established in class, where I first laid the historical groundwork, which enabled me to first foster greater understanding and mutual appreciation among my students.

CHAPTER I
A Holocaust?

FOR THE VAST majority of black students, the idea that indigenous peoples of Africa had a hand in their own condition of involuntary servitude was offensive, repulsive and often difficult to accept. To a certain extent to acknowledge this concept is to admit complicity and ultimately some degree of responsibility in one's own role in being relegated to the status of chattel slavery and its introduction to the North American continent. Intertribal conflict among Africa's coastal and interior tribes has long been a fixture of that continent and often has resulted in captured prisoners of war being relegated to, and placed within, the constraints of slavery. This was standard practice of European history as well. It can be traced back to the ancient Egyptians, Greeks and even the Romans, with slavery incorporated in aspects of warfare or as institutional entities (McKay, Hill, & Buckler, 1996, p.183). What was lacking, however, in the European or ancient models of slavery, especially vis-à-vis warfare, was the built in racial element so profound and evident in the North American realm. To the ancients the condition of slavery was simply regarded as more of a circumstance of misfortune than to any suggestion of racial inferiority. Within the African system, captured slaves (prisoners of war) were corralled by tribal factions (McKay, Hill, & Buckler, 1996, p. 183), and afterwards expedited to coastal regions where Europeans eagerly awaited the arrival of this most precious and profitable cargo (Norton, Katzman, Blight, Chudacoff, Paterson, Tuttle, & Escott, 2001, p. 74). Tribal African chieftains and Europeans alike participated in, and similarly profited from, this trans-Atlantic enterprise in human flesh.

Indentured servitude (a system of compensated slavery among poor white Europeans) had long since existed in North America. It ultimately proved unprofitable and increasingly politically sensitive as the Eighteenth century unfolded in the newly established American colonies (Norton, et al. 2001, p. 946). African cargo provided a more feasible and lucrative system in which to fuel the increasingly competitive capitalistic and global forces then vying for their share of newly emerging and established markets. It took European resources and innovation to turn fragmented African tribal warfare practices into a burgeoning industry and engine of commerce, but what is abundantly clear is that Africans facilitated Europeans, or at the very least actively aided those (Europeans) in their wholesale attempt to enslave fellow Africans.

Throughout North America, the Caribbean and adjacent areas, the African population began to swell and the institution of slavery itself began to assume the guiles of racism, as black codes and statutes were implemented as a means to ensure white control and supremacy in the face of these growing numbers. This delineation of rigid and often oppressive codes of conduct became necessary lest a repeat of the rampaging hoards and gangs of former slaves that occurred in ancient Roman times be repeated in the New World itself. Attitudes of racial superiority were then reinforced, and the system itself assumed the characteristics of institutionalism.

While the institution of slavery may be a matter of past relevance, the issue at hand is whether or not we can plausibly consider the institution of slavery a holocaust. In contemporary historical circles it has indeed become increasingly regarded as such. Arguably the impetus for just such delineation is largely being advanced by the African American community. It has been my own sense from independent reading and observation of student opinions that in order for the issue of slavery and the related journey across the Atlantic to be elevated to the status of genocide or holocaust is to acknowledge on the international stage the utter devastation wrought by this unprecedented human tragedy. Many whites regard the use of the term "holocaust" as a precursor to a potential admission of implied liability, leading ultimately then to the possibility of entitlements or even litigation. To be sure, the numbers are staggering and whether the pain, suffering and indignation heaped upon an entire race can or cannot be calculated, it is estimated that perhaps as many as fifteen million souls may have made the maligned voyaged now commonly referred to as the "middle passage," and that between one and two million may have perished during it (Franklin & Moss, 2000, p. 46).

The voyage itself was a nightmare beyond recognition, lasting weeks or even months. People were chained, restrained, and packed like human cargo, sometimes stacked in successive levels. Cargo holds were dark, air deprived and stagnant, with temperatures reaching well into the triple digits. Africans who often spoke different tribal languages were unable to communicate and lay languishing in collective human waste. There were the incessant and pitiful cries of children separated from their parents with destinations unknown.

Later, slave boat captains, in an attempt to improve their net worth, would learn to improve the overall appearance of their most precious cargo. (Much like fattening cattle prior to slaughter.) They would force feed Africans, utilizing mechanical devices to aid them in their efforts. These poor unfortunates were frequently roused above deck, chained together and forced to exercise in an attempt to thwart off the effects of atrophy. Occasionally despondent blacks would jump overboard in desperate attempts at suicide, often dragging those attached by chain with them (Norton, et al. 2001, p. 74). In some instances they were devoured by sharks often to the delight of white crews and deck hands. Prior to arrival on the North American side, these human commodities were systematically cleaned and prepared for sale as hair was colored, teeth painted and skin oiled in order to extenuate muscle tone. In every way these practices mimicked patterns used by horse traders making African chattel slavery commensurate with that of the handling of livestock.

In an original book in my possession entitled <u>Cabinet of Freedom</u> published in 1836 by the British government, which was at that time holding hearings regarding abandoning the slave trade, numerous testimonies given before Parliament are recounted that provide a most poignant depiction of the atrocities espoused within that industry. One slave ship captain in particular named Frazer was accused of holding hot coals to the mouth of a slave who refused to eat. Another captain forced the separation of a ten-month-old baby from his African mother. When the infant would not respond to forced feeding the captain ordered the child's foot to be dipped in hot oil, whereby the skin and nails of the baby began to peel off (Clarkson, 1836). Still the baby did not respond, and within approximately one hour, the infant died. To add insult to injury, the grieving mother was forced to take her lifeless offspring and dispose of him into the depths of the ocean. Another poignant depiction was found in the testimony of a river boat captain on the African river Namibia, who had previously told his pilot that he needed a cabin boy to act as his personal assistant. Shortly thereafter, the pilot steered the vessel to a nearby dock where two young African boys were selling vegetables. Believing them to be about the right age for the above duty, the pilot proceeded to kidnap the two youths, who presumably never again saw their families (Clarkson, 1836).

For much of white and Christian Europe of the sixteenth, seventeenth and eighteenth centuries, the human factor apparently never entered into the equation. This component may have been the last manifestation of the commercial revolution and these poor souls lacking in the principals of proclaimed superior Christian ideals provided the impetus necessary to secure advantage in an ever shrinking and increasingly competitive geo-political sphere. In a world population not yet even approaching one billion people, the African slave trade and colonization of the continent by competitive and rival European powers, wrought the utmost devastation perhaps ever inflicted upon any geographical region. Disease, tribal warfare, economic depredation, and the draining of Africa's best and most talented populations (not to mention subsequent European colonization) have caused Africa to reel, and to never sufficiently recover. Ascribing blame to any particular ethnic group might prove not only counter-productive but nearly impossible as well. The Portuguese, Spanish, English, French, North Americans, South Americans and many others, including Africans, had a role in the affair, blurring responsibility.

Genocide as described in the Webster's New World Dictionary refers to "the systematic killing of, or a program of action intended to destroy a whole national or ethnic group." That same publication goes on to describe a holocaust as "great or total destruction of life, especially by fire." And while I cannot say whether the Trans-Atlantic Slave Trade, with all of its associated atrocities, meets the criterion of genocide or even that of a holocaust, it does nonetheless at least appear to approach the threshold. White students, who have no direct or implied complicity in the affair, I believe on some vicarious level, harbor at least some residual misgivings. For blacks, by and large, not only do the middle passage and the practice of slavery approach the "threshold," it discernibly crosses over it.

In some respects, when examining this epic scenario of human tragedy, it seems as though there can be no going back. In other instances, going forward on this matter seems impossible as well. Perhaps continuing on the path of sustained and consummate dialogue will allow for lateral movement, or at least a greater degree of compassion and perhaps comprehension between the races. Students of both races seemed equally appalled by the humiliation and indignity of this most egregious act of history, but African American students in particular found it difficult to accept their own ancestral complicity in the affair, and many to this day probably still refuse to accept this historically proven premise.

CHAPTER II

An Accident of History

ANYONE WHO LIVES in the greater metropolitan area of Buffalo has a consummate appreciation for the manner in which a single moment in time can dramatically alter the course of human events. On the fourth of September, 1901, President William McKinley and his presidential entourage rolled into the city of Buffalo only to be greeted by a twenty one gun salute which resulted in the shattering of the train's windows, small and numerous cuts and abrasions, as well as the First Lady being administered with smelling salts. The next morning of the 5th, the President visited nearby Niagara Falls, and later that day attended Buffalo's internationally renowned Pan-American Exposition. It was here, while visiting the Temple of Music exhibition, that McKinley was shot twice by anarchist assassin Leon Czolgosz, where he (Czolgosz)was subsequently wrestled to the ground by James Parker, "a Herculean negro" as books of the period then referred to him (Reed, 1901). Vice President Theodore Roosevelt was summoned to Buffalo, where he was sworn in as the nation's 26th President (less than two miles from the college itself), ushering in a new period of American expansion and increased international involvement. Additionally, four successive Super bowl appearances, the phrase "wide right", still resonates heavily on the conscience of the city's hard scrabble sports fans, as does the epic phrase, "no goal", relative to the Buffalo Sabres appearance of the

1999 Stanley Cup finals. Moreover, a Blizzard which inundated the same region in January of 1977 has left Buffalo with a bruised psyche and a damaged reputation as the snow capital of the nation, one from which the city has yet to recover from.

Sometimes events in history can be determined by the most subtle of nuances or anomalies, but whose true impact is not realized for generations. One man in particular represents this enigmatic and sometimes obscure historical phenomenon, and he emerges in the form of Eli Whitney, a New England inventor and educator. His relative effect was to forever alter the course of human events in the most profound manner, which at the time was neither intended nor even anticipated.

After the initial success of America's War for Independence (1775-1781) and the subsequent failure of our first attempt at united government (Articles of Confederation 1777), the thirteen colonies gathered at Annapolis and later again at Philadelphia, in order to architect a more perfect attempt at union. Recognizing the shortcomings of the Articles of Confederation, attempts were made to strengthen and to create a more centralized form of federated government. Among these was to forego state's rights in favor of a strong executive (president) and a federal legislative body (congress) in order to provide more aptly from a common defense and to further expedite our commercial expansion. Most were in agreement of these basic precepts, but the South was reluctant to provide for any greater degree of federal control at the expense of state's rights.

Moreover, the touchy subject of slavery threatened to unravel all achieved up to that point in the summer of 1787, as it was predetermined that for a government operating under a constitution a required majority approval of nine of the thirteen states would be necessary to effect its establishment. Any or all attempts to disband or to destroy the institution of slavery would only cause the Southern colonies to balk at the proposed Constitution. In order to ameliorate the situation, a compromise was reached designed to facilitate Southern acceptance. Commonly referred to as the "Three-Fifths compromise" the South was permitted to retain its institution of slavery and, for purposes of taxation and representation, a slave (whose work was deemed to be 60 percent of the intrinsic value of a working free person), would constitute two-thirds of a free person in representational value (Norton, et al., 2001, p. 188). In addition, it was further agreed that in 20 years (presumably in 1808); Congress would be enabled to permanently outlaw the slave trade through the legal abolishment of direct slave importation to this nation from external sources. Then perhaps the institution might begin either to abate or perhaps even to die of natural causes.

From a Northern perspective (most Northern states were in the process of abolishing or eliminating this practice altogether) this seemed amenable, given that for all relative purposes the slave trade would come to expire in less than a generation. From the Southern point of view, many believed they had duped their Northern counterparts, as in the South most anticipated a continuation of the slave practice through successive and long-term breeding programs. In fact, some came to regard the state of Virginia as a veritable "baby-making factory" for African Americans.

However, at the dawn of the 19th century, the prevailing economic climate began to intimate that the days of slavery as a viable social and economic institution might well be nearing an end. While cotton and tobacco reigned supreme, in much of the South these industries were labor intensive, subject to weather patterns and the former, in particular, extraordinarily tough on the soil. In some instances, after only a couple of years of intensive cotton production a plantation's soil base may have been sufficiently deteriorated or minerally depleted so as to preclude further planting of this most profitable commodity. The feeding clothing and providing of even basic medical care and the providing of rudimentary housing for the slaves caused some in the South to anticipate the possible mitigation of this once profitable practice. Some Southerners sought to push westward in search of more fertile ground but this practice only added additional costs to the overall production of cotton, particularly for the short-staple variety often grown in the more interior areas. To some it seemed the days of abundant cotton production and the very institution of slavery, on which its pillars rested, were indeed possibly numbered.

Then, at the end of the 1700's, almost as if by an accident of history, a New England inventor and educator would forever thereafter dramatically alter the course of world events.

Eli Whitney, a classical Yankee in every sense of the word, would be thrust upon the world stage, almost unintentionally. As a young boy growing up in Massachusetts during the Revolution, he was by all accounts both curious and cantankerous. He operated a small nail manufacturing enterprise from his father's workshop at a time when British embargo of this valuable commodity interfered with the day-to-day operations of local farming industries and the small surrounding New England villages. While attempting to save money for college in order to study at the prestigious Yale School of Law,

Whitney worked as a laborer, performed odd tasks. He even accepted work as a school teacher. Due in part to financial constraints, the young Eli, responding to a newspaper ad, was compelled to seek a teaching position as a private tutor for a well-to-do South Carolina planter. After negotiating a predetermined contract fee, Whitney secured passage on a vessel and headed south towards his destination. While on that journey, Eli came into contact with the family and widow of former Revolutionary War General and quasi-national hero, Nathanial Green, who was in command during the great conflict of General Washington's southern armies. The widow Green took an almost immediate liking to the young educator, even extending an invitation for him to join her at the Green plantation in Mulberry, Georgia, should his anticipated teaching job in South Carolina not be to his liking ("Interactive Eli Whitney Biography," n.d.). Whitney arrived at his designation only to find the agreed upon wages to be in discrepancy. Refusing to be manipulated, Eli proceeded to make his way to the Green estate, deciding to accept instead the hospitality of the widow Green. To repay the kindness of Mrs. Green, Eli, ever the tinker, often made small repairs while a guest at the residence (Norton, et al. 2001, p. 196).

One evening while entertaining visitors at the estate, Mrs. Green was said to have overheard the lamentations of several gentlemen farmers, who in typical fashion of the day were engaged in a discourse regarding the unprofitable nature of their once burgeoning agricultural enterprises, namely cotton production. (Norton, et al. 2001). Almost as a means by which to emphasize pride in her esteemed Northern visitor, the widow Green suggested, "Gentlemen, apply to my friend Mr. Whitney, he can make anything." (Norton, et al., 2001, p 195). Whitney must have cringed, being put on the spot and then taken to the task in such an abrupt fashion. The response of the Southern gentlemen must have been commensurate with "How about it Yankee boy? Ya'll are supposed to be so smart, surely you can develop something." Knowing in all probability the task would be nearly impossible, and further hoping the young Northerner would fall flat on his face. Eli, not timid in the least, probably interpreted the affair as a personal challenge to his abilities, integrity and overall character. At the behest of Mrs. Green and her fiancé, Phineas Miller, Whitney observed firsthand the processes of hand grooming cotton and the painstaking process of removing the intertwined seeds. Eli was invited to utilize the Green's workshop and all of its contained tools. He began to work out details and subsequently hammered out a working prototype which ultimately was completed in only ten day's time.

Affixing a crank to two separate rollers with attached teeth in order to groom the seeds from the fiber, Whitney attached a box and screen below to catch the disassociated seeds. A series of brushes turning in opposite directions served to continuously clean the brushes and to rid them of fiber and other debris. Simple in construction and brilliant in design, Whitney's "cotton gin" was presented to his Southern hosts. It must have been received with chagrin and simultaneous exaltation as the "Yankee boy" succeeded beyond anyone's wildest expectations. The device was kept under lock and key and placed in the Green's workshop. It was Whitney's intention to patent his invention, but within days the workshop was broken into, and shortly thereafter crude and rudimentary replicas could be found throughout the adjacent areas. Imitation maybe the utmost form of flattery, but to Whitney, it represented the loss of any potential financial windfall that might have resulted from his genius. Nonetheless, he pursued the patent process in March of 1797, but through litigation and rival claims of similar inventions, the official license and patent was not granted until 1807. By then working prototypes of the device were found to be commonplace throughout the Deep South.

As for the cleverness of the "cotton gin" the overall affect was to preserve the viability of a dying or at least stagnant cotton industry. It was said of the device's productivity that it improved production from 3,135 bales of cotton in 1790 (before the cotton gin) to 1,346,232 within fifty years (Phillips, 2010, Table 2).

If true, the ratio was indeed staggering and revolutionary and, therefore, all but insured the perpetuity of both the cotton industry and the institution of slavery necessary to support it. Cotton would extend westward into the Trans Mississippi, Alabama, Louisiana and points west, simultaneously extending the range of slavery as well. The political and cultural ramifications of Whitney's invention could not have been known then or even reasonably anticipated. Through legislation, as well as economic and market forces, slavery had been perhaps doomed to expire or even to die a natural death. But attributed largely to the efforts of Eli Whitney (who went on to promote mass production and interchangeable parts), the institution of slavery expanded as cotton became king, and the Southern economy became inextricably linked with its propagation and success. The argument can be made that the empire of cotton even helped fuel the war with Mexico (1846-48) in an attempt to secure additional western lands. Irrespective, it would take a civil war, the death of six hundred thousand souls, and an untold number of casualties, as well as another 70 years, before institution of slavery would be abrogated; and therefore, an entire race would be emancipated in the most violent and non-complaisant manner.

To me the question has always been, in retrospect, would Whitney either circumvent or disavow his invention of the cotton gin altogether, had he known of its impending social and political repercussions? If you embrace the precept that for every action, there is an equal and opposite reaction, then Whitney's advancement of the principles of mass production through its interchangeable parts, helped to expand the Northern economy into a manufacturing one, which ultimately then (1861-65) used its production capacity and might to destroy the Southern economy, way of life and cherished institutions including slavery. Most of my students, black or white, harbored little if any animosity towards Whitney's direct role in the whole affair. In fact, they seemed to regard his role as inculpable, or even perhaps simply an accident of history.

CHAPTER III

The Road to Emancipation

ON THE FRIDAY following the 2008 election of Barack Obama, a cartoon appeared in <u>USA Today</u> (November 2008) depicting Dr. Martin Luther King placing his hand on the right shoulder of the President Elect, and Abraham Lincoln placing his hand on the left shoulder, presumably congratulating the President Elect and illuminating their own role in the long march towards racial equality in America. (Strangely and perhaps in an odd twist of irony the lineage of our nation's first black President provides him with no link to our nation's history of slavery.) The illustration, while touching, is hardly reflective of events as they truly transpired. To students of my African American classes and to most in general, our nation's 16th President is often viewed as the Great Emancipator, who through his magnanimous character and beneficent spirit sought to free an entire race from the bondage of slavery. Equally misconstrued among the vast majority of my students, was their rather rudimentary understanding of the Emancipation Proclamation and Lincoln's implied role in the freeing of African Americans from centuries of forced subjugation. President Lincoln was not a particular admirer of the African American race nor was he an advocate for black rights. Above all, Lincoln was a masterful politician. Emancipation of blacks from the condition of involuntary servitude was a social and economic means to a political end. In fact, the martyred President stated explicitly that could the preservation of the Union be achieved through the maintenance of the maligned institution of slavery that would be preferable to affording freedom to the slaves.

By 1862, Lincoln had far more pressing issues, including the prosecution of the war itself, than the emancipation of the slaves. None was more important than preventing potential European (English and French) intervention on behalf of the Confederacy. It seemed the Confederacy was, dangerously close to obtaining this lofty diplomatic coup. The English and the French were making direct overtures indicating their possible intercession and formal recognition of the Confederate States of America (Flato, 1970, p. 89). Such recognition would have likely resulted in the demise of the American Union. With British forces stationed just north of the U.S. border in Canada and French forces located south of Texas, in a puppet Mexican state, Lincoln indeed had immense cause for concern. Additionally, Lincoln faced the potential repercussions of combined Anglo and French naval operations off the Atlantic coast, possibly even disrupting or circumventing his own Union naval blockade of all Southern ports. It is probably correct to assert that the only thing preventing European assistance to the rebellious Confederate cause was the very institution of slavery itself.

Confederate officials were repeatedly advised through Anglo and French diplomatic sources to abandon the maligned institution as a precursor to any official recognition of the rebel cause or mutual cooperation, but it was to no avail. England and France had formally and legally abandoned the practice of slavery, due in part to geographical location, fledgling worker movements (which viewed slavery as competition and the reason for prevailing low wages) and political or religious reforms.

Lincoln, ever the opportunist, saw an opportunity to trump possible Anglo French intervention by appearing at least to abolish slavery on paper, if not by conscience. The Emancipation Proclamation called for the cessation of slavery in areas not yet controlled by Union forces, and yet simultaneously allowed for its continued existence in the border states such as Kentucky and Maryland where Federal forces were already active (Foote, 1974, p. 89). In reality, however, it freed almost no slaves, and only hinted to, or anticipated the eventual abolishment of the practice in the Deep South, if the Confederacy did not lay down its arms. A line in the sand was being drawn, which, if crossed by the South, there could be no return. What the Lincoln administration had in fact done, however, was to issue a blank check for the emancipation of the slaves, that could be cancelled should the need arise, not fully anticipating that one day that check might indeed, have to be cashed. Irrespective, the Union at least on paper stood for the abolishment of the institution and that was sufficient to thwart full blown European intervention, because the French and British could no longer pitch to their constituency cart blanch assistance for a Confederate cause that both advanced and supported the unpopular institution of slavery. Lincoln has been heretofore regarded as the "great" emancipator in the eyes of many African Americans (including most of my students), yet this title is misleading, or at the very least, less than reflective of true and actual events.

When in fact the Emancipation Proclamation check was cashed, and the Confederacy was brutally and forcefully subjugated, the nation as a whole found itself facing a dilemma of epic proportions. What to do with the wholesale displacement of over four million African Americans recently relinquished from the bonds of slavery (Franklin & Moss, 2000, p. 258). Lacking entirely political organization, illiterate (in fact only 1 in 4 white Southerners at the time could read at functional levels), and nearly devoid of any marketable skills, African Americans were indeed in a conundrum. The initial Lincoln plan and upon his subsequent death in April of 1865, was to ship as many African Americans as possible to the western and northern realms of their indigenous homeland in Africa (Franklin & Moss, 2000, p. 249). This proved nearly impossible almost from the beginning; due in part to matters of logistics and financing. Millions of former slaves, many of whom were still searching for lost loved ones (ads appeared for decades thereafter in newspapers, circulars and periodicals), could no longer identify with the customs of their homeland, and could not find the wherewithal to embrace such an apparently ill-conceived concept (Franklin & Moss, 2000, p. 253). The complete disruption of an entire social class and its ramifications thereof, were fully unintended and again almost completely unanticipated. The majority white community either lacked the political will or the social resolve to address the issue at hand. An entire enclave of American society was in limbo and the subsequent ineptness of the Johnson administration (Andrew Johnson was no Abraham Lincoln), and the latent hostility of a radical Republican Congress towards that administration did little to alleviate the problem (Norton et al., 2001, p. 436). Johnson, in fact, in his annual message of 1867 to that body went on to suggest that Blacks possessed less "capacity for government than any other race of people. No independent government of any form has ever been successful in their hands; . . . wherever they have been left to their own devices they have shown a constant tendency to relapse into barbarism." (Norton, et.al.2001, Vol.1, p. 436) Johnson's views were not entirely out of sequence with those of the majority of white Americans. One Georgia newspaper in 1866 asserted, "most of the white citizens believe that the institution of slavery was right, and . . . they will believe that the condition, which comes nearest to slavery that can now be established will be the best." (Norton, et.al.2001, Vol.2, p. 445)

Congress, however, did manage to advance numerous policies and legislation in an attempt to remediate existing conditions. Among these were the Thirteenth Amendment (forever legally ending the practice of slavery in America) and the Fourteenth Amendment (conferring citizenship upon blacks, and prohibiting states from "abridging" their constitutional rights). The Reconstruction Act of 1867 further punished the South by dividing it into five districts of military occupation, but also contained refinements to the existing Freedman's Bureau, which was initially designed to aid former slaves as well as poor whites, whose relative status had been relegated to that of refugees due to the ravages of the Civil War.

One evening during a lecture, I was attempting to convey themes relative to the Freedman's Bureau, and was rather surprised by the degree of alacrity displayed by the students concerning this matter. Among the Bureaus concepts was its promise to provide displaced slaves with a helping hand by utilizing a component commonly referred to as "40 acres and a mule" (Norton et al., 2001, p. 428). In theory, so that freed slaves might be able to economically take care of themselves, blacks were to be the recipients, at the behest of the Federal government, of 40 acres and a mule, as well as tools with which to begin small and self-sustaining farming enterprises. The impetus being that former slaves would no longer need to be the wards of local, state or federal governments if they possessed the means required to provide for themselves. In practice, however, relatively few blacks received any such allowances. One student interceded that all would be forgiven if, in order to make right this former egregious behavior, the federal government, and the people of the United States, would now make good on that initial promise. Another black student followed up that with "as a matter of fact, the government could keep the mule, if it would just provide us with the promised 40 acres." An immediate retort from the white side of the class was that blacks had already been more than amply compensated by other programs including "welfare, food stamps, and free college grants." Clearly racial lines were being drawn in the classroom with a preponderance of white students concurring with this latest verbal slur.

The tension was further exacerbated when I introduced an additionally contentious topic. At the close of the millennium, I offered, a member of Congress had advanced for discussion on the floor the concept of a possible one time reparation or payment for past wrongs and injustices inflicted upon African Americans during the period of slavery (Hall, 2000, Resolution 356). White students were vociferous and immediate in their condemnation of any and all such plans. Black students, conversely generally lent their wholehearted support to the idea, believing it would be belated justice. Admittedly, however, several of the majority disagreed, suggesting that this would only further inflame existing hostility between the races. The attitude of students on either side of the aisle was quite readily discernible, and their immediate assertion was that the advocate of any such legislation must have been an African American member of Congress. But in truth, the proposal was advanced by a white legislator who simply wanted the issue between the races to be dealt with accordingly, in order that we, as a nation, might somehow put this behind us and move forward. White students asserted that a program of such magnitude could not effectively or judiciously be carried out. I reminded them, however, of similar plans of restitution including that afforded to victims of Japanese internment during World War II, and their respective surviving families. Similar payouts have been afforded survivors of the holocaust and as an added element reminded them that in fact the mid-Atlantic slave trade has increasingly come to be regarded as a holocaust in and of its own right.

Additional thoughts were advanced and infused into the conversation. Who would receive such benefits? And who could prove lineage and a direct link to their slave descendants? All of which would prove to be a logistical nightmare. The greatest resentment came from the minority of white students who reasserted this historical tragedy was not of their making and as such they were in no way responsible. Moreover, they continued the whole affair was a transgression based in history and therefore, has no contemporary relevance or bearing on the future and should be dismissed outright.

As the discussion grew more heated, I interjected a question of my own. Who, I asked, was going to provide me and my family with federal restitution? There was a momentary pause, followed by the almost uniform inquiry as to why my family ought to be restituted. My great-great-great-grandfather, I stated, fought for the Union (Vermont) and was captured during the conflict, ultimately being remanded to a Confederate prison camp. It has been estimated that one out of every four Union soldiers incarcerated by Confederate authorities did not return to his home due to deplorable camp conditions and the inherent shortages of food, material and resources of a dying Confederacy. Therefore, I contended my great-great-great grandfather, as a man who fought for the Union, and ultimately the cause of black freedom, and who presumably suffered at the hands of his Confederate captors, ought as well to be compensated. This comment solicited almost no response from the African American student body. It appears that the lines of restitution and reparation may be sufficiently blurred so as to be its ultimate demise. This, however, in no way diminishes the legacy of pain, suffering and indignation experienced by African Americans over the preceding decades and centuries. I will at the end of this expose, offer what I believe to be an appropriate substitution for what has become known as the program of reparation or restitution.

Irrespective of the means, the abrupt manner in which the accelerated and forced integration of the black race into mainstream American was effected all but insured that the road to equality and relative coexistence between the races would be a long and protracted one. The extent to which residual animosities and latent hostilities continue to resonate among my students provides clear evidence of a continued journey, and that the nation's rendezvous with its presupposed destiny, and espoused racial harmony, lies yet ahead of us.

CHAPTER IV

The Great Debate

FOLLOWING THE TUMULTUOUS period of the Civil War and the era of Reconstruction, blacks ultimately faced another immense dilemma: how to win white approval in a predominantly white society. African Americans, who only recently threw off the shackles of slavery, and who were regarded as property commensurate to that of sheep and cattle, could ill expect to be greeted with open arms by the white majority.

Poor white Southerners (sometimes today referred to as white trash) disdained the notion that blacks could be viewed with any sense of parity. Poor whites immersed in poverty could always respond with the powerful phrase, "At least I'm not a nigger." In many ways it was a built-in safety net preventing poor whites from falling to the lowest realm of the social scrap heap of America. In fact, all across the South, and in other regions, codes were adopted to ensure that blacks would never ascend any higher in social rank than that of the country's labor force. Even our Nations first vagrancy laws have their roots in the African American experience as a means to ensure that blacks could not remain idle or unemployed, lest they be subject to arrest at the hands of local authorities (Norton et al., 2001 p. 437). In addition, and as a method to further ensure that the workforce did not remain idle, the system of *sharecropping* was implemented throughout the Deep South. Former slaves were compelled by whatever means to seek employment on terms less than advantageous to their overall economic well-being. In theory, if not in practice, it was better to work on a former Georgia plantation in a sharecropping capacity, than it was to serve ten years in a Georgia State penitentiary or to work on a chain gang. African Americans again were reacquainted with their former slave quarters. In order to furnish these quarters, blacks were extended the ability, via a payment plan, to purchase amenities they could ill afford from the company store, which more often than not, was owned by their former masters. Extending such credit was a means by which to keep blacks in perpetual poverty, and permanently tied to the land (Norton, et al., 2001, p. 434). Any attempt to leave the land prior to payment in full of all accrued debts would result in arrest. By the 1880's, blacks were once again operating as forced labor in a form of quasi-slavery within the sharecropping system.

Most African Americans began to believe that achieving any degree of parity or perceived co-existence with the white race would be a long and arduous task. Ideas on just how to achieve this status were abound. Many focused on the perspectives of two of the most renowned and yet diametrically opposed points of view, put forth by two equally divergent personalities of the late nineteenth and early twentieth century's: Booker T. Washington and W.E.B. Du Bois. These men came from two distinctly different backgrounds. They would ultimately emerge as the voice and conscience of generations of African Americans to follow. In my lectures, their perspectives on matters of race, attitudes, and the ultimate direction of the black movement resonate to this day, and continue to inflame and invoke the most heated of discussions.

Booker T. Washington was a man of modest means and perhaps best known for his widely read Up From Slavery. He grew up as a young boy on a Virginia plantation in the late 1850's. By all accounts he was a young man of great intellectual capacity and drive, and thus after emancipation he managed to acquire a spotty education. Later he attended the prestigious Hampton Institute of Washington. Showing great initiative, he made his way to the school hungry and penniless, at times even sleeping under porches, all along the way performing odd tasks. Upon arrival, he was told that he did not have the initial required tuition and, therefore, could not expect to attend. Undaunted, he argued that he could perform janitorial duties in order to pay the tuition, while simultaneously pursuing his studies. Discipline and education he believed were the keys to success in a white man's world. Later on, and based on this philosophy Booker T. would go on to create the Tuskegee Institute of Alabama, a school designed to elevate his race utilizing the aforementioned core values. Tuskegee focused overwhelmingly on the trades and agricultural processes, skills which Booker T. believed would provide the greatest dividends and, yet, simultaneously would be the least offensive to whites. Carpentry, masonry and agriculture would form the basis by which his entire race could pull themselves up by their bootstraps and gradually earn them acceptance into the racial mosaic of American society. Inherent to this theory was the idea that if blacks could be thrifty and patient, and keep their "eyes on the prize," they would one day prevail and win white acceptance and approval.

As a black institute in the Deep South during the 1880's, Tuskegee by all accounts had somehow managed to foster good relations with the surrounding community including the white members, who even solicited services and materials from the school in order to facilitate trade and advance commerce. As head of the institute, Booker T. even performed spot bed checks and provided lessons in bathing and the brushing of teeth, basic skills he believed necessary in promoting pride in one's appearance and thus in one's self. Students often grew their own food. And through acquired skills and learning, they even constructed many of the buildings on the grounds of the Institute. With their newly learned skills and tools, Booker T. believed the black race could make its way in a white man's world. Through successive generations of hard work, blacks would then, and only then, achieve social and economic status in a manner non-threatening to the predominate white culture, thereby earning its respect. As a means of promoting racial harmony and conciliating whites, Booker T. suggested in his much celebrated speech at the World's Fair in Atlanta in 1895 that "in all things that are purely social we can be as separate as the five fingers, yet one as the hand in all things essential to mutual progress" (Washington, 1901, p. 221-222).

Some of my students nodded approvingly, others displayed their apparent displeasure, and yet the cross section of emotions did not appear to manifest along racial lines. I continued by suggesting that it was Booker T's intent that through hard work, thrift and patience that the black race could elevate itself by laying the very economic and vocational cornerstones necessary on which to construct a solid foundation for future social and economic progress. Moreover, it was not that Booker T. disdained the advanced studies of the humanities or sciences, but rather he believed more substantial returns or dividends were to be found in his doctrine than in the pursuits of academia, which in the end, would only prove to be antagonistic or inflammatory to the majority of whites.

Later after the turn of the century, Booker T. was extended an invitation to dine at the White House, with President Theodore Roosevelt. The President, upon making the gesture, became the recipient of the most spiteful and acrimonious letters and threats perhaps ever afforded a Chief Executive of the United States. The President afterwards, in a manner designed to thumb his nose at these resounding racial pundits, later explained to the Press that seldom had he had such an enlightening and delightfully entertaining experience as when he dined with the most captivating Booker T. Washington.

Strangely enough this more tempered position of Booker T. did not invoke the animosity from my African American students that I would have predicted or anticipated. It appeared to me, that a number of black students found some elements of truth or even kernels of wisdom in this doctrine, at least in the historical context in which it occurred. As a general rule, white students argued that in its overall context, Booker T.'s philosophy and actions probably followed a correct and prudent course, given that blacks only decades before were regarded as property, and therefore could not realistically expect white acceptance and equality without first having "earned it."

W. E. B. Du Bois, however, represented altogether the other end of the spectrum for most African Americans and white students. Born in Massachusetts (far above the Mason Dixon line) Du Bois was neither in proximity, nor exposed to the pervasive and sometimes overt discrimination seen in the South. It is not to say that Du Bois did not experience racism, but rather the degree of severity compared to that experienced by Booker T. must have been nominal. Du Bois, a scholar in every respect, completed his undergraduate studies at Fisk University, and became the first African American to secure his Doctorate of Philosophy degree at the prestigious Harvard University. Moreover, while studying abroad in Berlin, Du Bois had seen a culture more accepting towards blacks. It would probably be correct to assert that Du Bois' overall perspective on race relations were more cosmopolitan than those of Booker T.

While teaching at Atlanta University, however, Du Bois would become all too well-acquainted with the stark realities of Jim Crow, and the deeply entrenched system of racial inequality as it existed in the South. To Du Bois this revelation must have been appalling and especially alarming. Through a series of essays and publications, Du Bois began to assail the basic components and foundations of the preeminently popular Booker T. Du Bois believed Booker's doctrines actually worked to the overall detriment of the black race. Booker T's "Atlanta Exposition Speech" was openly touted by Du Bois as the "Atlanta Compromise" in which Du Bois suggested the racial inferiority of blacks was affirmed in an effort to be conciliatory to whites both Northern and Southern (Franklin & Moss, 2000, p. 305). In this regard, it seemed to Du Bois that Booker T. had become the "poster child" for the white classes who sought to maintain and perpetuate their systems of social, political and moral superiority over their black brethren. Du Bois espoused that not through hard work, perseverance and respectfulness would the African American race achieve parity, but rather through the systematic pursuit of education and intelligence and an overall awareness of their circumstances. Through these things, blacks could begin to manipulate the forces around them, thus leading to their overall betterment and advantage. In this manner, and according to his own "Talented Tenth" doctrine, Du Bois believed blacks should educate themselves to their highest potential, and demonstrate that African Americans were every bit as intelligent and as capable as their white counterparts and, as such, would then begin to earn their respect (Franklin and Moss, 2000, p. 305-306). His posture was assertive and progressive at a time when nearly each and every day the lynching of a black man was reported somewhere in America.

Du Bois was also instrumental in what ultimately became the forerunner to the N.A.A.C.P., when he summoned a national convention to meet in the Niagara Frontier (the Niagara Movement) to address issues of race and a possible collective response or action. Upon his arrival, Du Bois attempted to solicit a hotel room in the city of Buffalo, he was curtly reminded that one was not available to a man of his complexion, and he was forced to cross the Niagara River to secure a hotel room in nearby Fort Erie, Canada. Articles published in his "Crisis" magazine served as a continual source of agitation to the white race and to those African Americans more inclined to embrace the more conciliatory tones of Booker T. Opinions solicited from my students relative to the issue of W.E.B. Du Bois were far less than neutral. At the dawn of a new century, and on the precipice of a new millennium, his proactive stance and incendiary tones still resonated among my students as inflammatory and to some extent exceedingly divisive. When I suggested that collective political organization is sometimes needed by minorities in order for their voices to be heard and accounted for, most of the white students argued that it was tantamount to organized black resistance to all things white, designed to ensure that the black cause would have a leg up, or at least some degree of unfair leverage or advantage.

While its inception (N.A.A.C.P.) may have been more or less innocuous, its construed existence seems less than "making friends with white neighbors in every way" as advocated by Booker T. Washington (Washington, 1901). Regardless of the divergent views expressed by both Booker T. Washington, and W.E.B. Du Bois following the turmoil of the Civil War era, African Americans found themselves in a dilemma of epic proportions. And while these two widely respected and divergent points of view became beacons for an entire race, just who offered the most prudent course in which to follow, remains to this day unresolved.

Finally in reference to the white students, who remarked that blacks needed to first earn the respect of the white community, before they could be accepted with any degree of racial parity into it, they appear in some aspects to embrace the central theme of Booker T. Washington's overall thesis. I must admit that as for myself, I am at times reticent to accept the premise, but it is, however, analogous to a component of my own life and to that of many parents of our nation at large. My own daughters, age 18 and 21 have come to embrace the concept that upon the magical and numerical age of 18, they have somehow become adults and simultaneously anticipate being treated as equals and generally expect me to respond accordingly. In many ways, this strangely mimic's the historical circumstances of the black race, which upon the magical date in 1863 were lead on the path of emancipation, but which could not have realistically expected widespread acceptance by a more entrenched and established white society. As for my daughters, whom I have raised for nearly two decades, educated, paid their expenses and generally nurtured, I still do not at this point look upon them as my equal. And at just what point I will do so, I cannot as of yet say, since I have earned college degrees, built most of my own house, worked two careers for nearly a quarter of a century and have suffered immense trials and tribulations.

In a similar vein and for the black community at large, Booker T.'s approach of earning the respect of the white establishment (which up to this point had either run, organized, or affected the financial, political and social structures and institutions under which the nation then operated), may indeed have been one of prudence. But the question remained at which juncture would that respect be "earned," and when could that "equality" reasonably be expected? This, of course, is precisely why the historical and racial issue itself probably has never been satisfactorily resolved.

CHAPTER V
Educational Foundations

WHEN ADDRESSING THE suburban college students in my twentieth century U.S. history classes, as a rule I try to incorporate several accomplished individual African Americans whom I believe have made a significant contribution and inroads to the overall development of our national character. I have already covered Booker T. Washington and W.E.B. Du Bois. Martin Luther King is now thankfully and routinely covered in elementary through senior high school curriculums. But there exists several other African Americans who should perhaps become introduced into those curriculums—Marcus Garvey, Paul Robeson, Jessie Owens, Joe Louis Barrow and Malcolm X—and therefore I systematically incorporate them into my own college level history programs.

Marcus Garvey provides enormous insight into the mores and status of issues relative to the races early in the twentieth century, which to some extent continues to resonate into the twenty-first century itself. Garvey, a man of immense physical stature and presence, indomitable spirit, and innate intelligence, possessed many of the attributes that a pervasively white and allegedly superior society perhaps feared most. Garvey came from Jamaica and a dominant "colored" culture. (Many Jamaicans do not even believe themselves to be black.) Garvey had managed a print shop, which placed him in continual proximity to the printed word, and afforded him the regular opportunity to expand both his oratorical and intellectual horizons. In 1916 he made his way to America and established the first North American office of the Universal Negro Improvement Association (U.N.I.A.), citing the need for self-determination within the black community. Creating organizations, para-military drill teams (sporting guns with uniforms of resplendent colors and large plumed hats of the most ostentatious variety), and a black nursing corps. Garvey (a bit of a peacock himself) thrived in his attempts to both organize and to agitate for what he called a "unity of all negro peoples of the world into one great body to establish a country and government of their own" presumably in either Liberia or perhaps even Ethiopia (Franklin & Moss, 2000, p. 395-398). A common and resonant theme in African American history, he advanced the concept of creating the Black Star Steamship Line (a racial spoof of the existing White Star Line), in order to facilitate and expedite an anticipated massive exodus of blacks from North America and other realms of the globe into those aforementioned regions of Africa. Growing up as a young man in the late 1960's and early 70's, I can still recall members of my own white community reiterating similar sentiments, which as it turns out, were indeed ideas rooted in actual historical precedent.

Garvey, obstinate, vociferous and fomenting to a fault, solicited through his "Negro World" and other venues, including the issuing and sale of stock for contributions in excess of ten million dollars, (a rather handsome and sizable amount in the 1920's), to advance the cause of "Negro Zionism" as it was then called (Franklin & Moss, 2000, p. 396). A man of this magnitude quickly drew the attention of local, state and federal authorities, who sometimes spied on his gatherings and speeches, hoping to seize on some treasonous or indictable commentary. (On occasion they used agents who painted their faces black.) This proved far more difficult than initially anticipated. In the end Federal authorities seized on a precedent (often used to arrest seemingly untouchable members of organized crime) and charged Garvey with mail fraud, in using that arm of the government to solicit for dollars and monies, which in some instances ultimately became unaccounted for. In the end, Marcus Garvey proved to be too reactionary, for even the vast majority of African Americans. He was imprisoned in 1925, later pardoned by President Coolidge, only later to be deported as an "undesirable alien."

To much of the collective student body, black or white, it appeared that Garvey and his sometimes contentious and often extreme practices proved too radical, doing little to advance the cause of racial harmony in America. Moreover, it seems, then as perhaps now, both races are often reluctant to embrace those elements which advocate sometimes aggressive, assertive, or even overtly proactive measures to achieve the lofty goal of equality.

Paul Robeson, a man of a mild demeanor and a more subtle countenance, remains a similarly interesting contributor to the early black movement of the twentieth century. Robeson, a contingent of the Harlem Renaissance then sweeping the region in the 1920's, has been ascribed as the first serious black actor and singer ever to play a leading role (opposite a white woman) in a prominent New York production (in 1924). Many thought Robeson's role was both inflammatory and scandalous, and that it might even precipitate racially motivated riots, which, incidentally, did not occur (Franklin & Moss, 2000, p. 420). Robeson, the son of a minister, was generally thought to be a quiet and introspective man, with a deep baritone voice. He was also highly regarded as an athlete and scholar; he went on to secure his law degree from Columbia University. At a time in the late 1920's when one of every two Americans attended the cinema at least once a week, Robeson, a uniquely gifted man, believed that he could best utilize his talents to elevate the stature of his race through theatre, motion pictures and the arts. In films ranging from D. W. Griffith's, <u>Birth of a Nation</u> or Al Jolson's 1927 talking picture, <u>The Jazz Singer,</u> and his black faced minstrel rendition of the song "Mammy," blacks had been consistently and systematically depicted and stereotyped in negative roles such as petty thieves, social delinquents and even sexually voracious predators. Mr. Robeson through his deep and projective voice, and stoic stature in productions such as the renowned, "Showboat," attempted to offset these negative depictions. He did so by portraying blacks from the vantage point of strength, vibrancy and one of character.

Traveling overseas, Robeson became a bit of an international celebrity, even going as far east as Russia, where he was greeted warmly (in part for political and propaganda purposes). Like many African Americans who traveled abroad, he found Europe to be largely devoid of the pervasive and overt racism so prevalent in America. Returning home must have only heightened his awareness and sensitivity towards all matters of race. By way of his educational background and the knowledge he gained from his extensive travels and broad experiences, which only reinforced his steadfast commitment to social matters, Robeson came to be regarded as a champion of the common man and a "citizen of the world." Observing other cultures, and being well-versed in the inherent mechanisms of racism fundamental to the social structure of America, he used his celebrity as a platform in which to bring to the forefront issues of social injustice. Admittedly at times his views incorporated elements of socialism and even occasionally flirted within the periphery of communist idealism. Given his broad experience and observational tendencies, Robeson could hardly be faulted for having skewed his views more to the political left. But due in part to these views, he earned the chagrin of the government and the more conservative political forces then operating in America. It was precisely these views which largely caused Robeson to become silenced during the infamous McCarthy era of the 1950's. Robeson disappeared from the public eye, only to re-emerge as a person with historic significance after his death in 1976. Paul Robeson, scholar, athlete, artist, activist and "citizen of the world" remains largely unknown and an enigma to students of either culture. Nonetheless, he was indispensable in keeping matters of social justice in the forefront, and relevant to the American political psyche.

The era of the 1930's was a unique and troubling time for the nation at large, but an especially hard one for African Americans in particular. As one black gentlemen of the period suggested blacks were already at the bottom of the social ladder, and as such did not have very far to fall before landing on the ground. In the throws of the Great Depression, with unemployment reaching a staggering 30%, and with the crumbling of the country's infrastructure and subsequent realignment of governmental institutions and social programs, America began to question the very principles on which it had come to be based (Norton et al., 2001, p. 707). In Europe and in Asia, the era of great dictators seemed to render the great democracies as either impotent, or increasingly unable to negotiate the great political and economic crises of their day. In America, the collapse of economic markets, the dust bowl, food riots, bread lines, and the disastrous Bonus March of 1932, seemed to underscore the fact that the days of our cherished institution of democracy might well be numbered. Conversely, in the midst of this great international climate of crisis, the great dictators such as Hitler, Mussolini, and Hirohito were able to stabilize and in some measure propel their economies, thus expanding their military and industrial bases. Moreover, particularly in the case of Adolf Hitler, these nations began to proclaim the racial superiority of their more homogeneous societies as the cause of their apparent cultural and societal advances. This may in fact be one of the lowest points in American history, a time like no other, whereby the nation was forced to re-assess, and to reexamine our history, core values, and relation to the rest of the world. With smaller nations in Europe and Asia being systematically leveraged, or in other instances swallowed up by the increasingly aggressive Axis powers, the reflection America saw of itself in the mirror could not have been a favorable one. It is in this, perhaps, the darkest of hours since the American Revolution or even the Civil War itself, that America's inherent strength and esteem would be rediscovered and salvaged by two unlikely heroes, both of African American decent: Jessie Owens and Joe Louis Barrow. In addressing my African American classes or even in my present American history courses, I can find almost no equivalent source of universal pride in race relations, than when the story of these two extraordinary sports figures is conveyed, and their significance and historical relevance is fully understood.

The 1936 Olympics were to be held in Hitler's Berlin, and were designed to be an international showcase of the self-proclaimed "master race." The substantial resources and talents of the Third Reich were systematically marshaled. Then they were implemented into national physical fitness programs. After which they were organized into a progressive and comprehensive Olympic strategy, designed to illustrate and to accentuate supposed Aryan superiority. The 1936 Depression conversely riddled the American Olympic teams. They faced, what must have seemed at the time, like insurmountable odds when they viewed their more technologically advanced German counterparts. In the midst of great economic paralysis, questions surfaced as to whether America could afford to send a team, much less expect to compete competitively. Seemingly, what was at stake was our nation's honor and its viability in a most politically unstable international atmosphere. The prospects did not look encouraging. America's relevance in the international realm was increasingly being called into question, and so too was the viability of our nation's institutions and system of government, and to some extent even its way of life. America's saving grace, however, was to be found in the form of a poor black boy, born to a sharecropping family in 1913 in a Deep South very influenced by Jim Crow and its restrictive institutions. Seeking economic opportunity, the Owens family made its way north to Cleveland, Ohio where Jessie, exhibiting early traits of thrift, hard work and perseverance, undertook numerous odd jobs to assist his family. He simultaneously attended public high school. It was while attending school that his talents for running became apparent. Realizing the boy's immense talent, the coach offered to train early in the mornings with Jessie, who could not train afternoons due to his after school jobs. Astoundingly, in his senior year of high school, Jesse ran the 100-yard dash in only 9.4 seconds, thus tying the existing world record ("Jesse Owens," n.d., para 5). In part because of his running ability, Jessie attended Ohio State University where he continued to pursue track and field, but at times when his collegiate team traveled, he and his fellow black colleagues were often denied admittance into hotels, restaurants and other venues.

Jessie went on to qualify for the 1936 U.S. Olympic team by once again breaking another world record in the 100-yard dash. The stage was later set that same year with hoards of the international media scheduled to coalesce in Berlin. The guest host Adolf Hitler and others continually boasted that Germany would indeed win the majority of medals. The assertion remained one of Aryan superiority over the inferiority of other races including Jews, Slavs, and Africans, who were sometimes referred to as "untermentions" or "sub-humans." Much to the embarrassment and chagrin of Hitler and to that of his Third Reich, Jessie went on to win four gold medals in the 100-meter, 200-meter, 4 x 100-meter relay and the long jump. In truth, the Germans did win the overall Olympic medal count but it was Jessie who emerged as the crescent star of the 1936 Olympic Games ("Jesse Owens," n.d., para. 2). Stories have surfaced about Hitler's refusal to shake hands with Jessie, but in fact after the first day of Olympic competition, Hitler, chose, as a matter of policy, to shake no additional hands, an option afforded him by the International Olympic Committee. In the end, it was the "inferior race," which had made a "monkey" of Hitler's self-proclaimed master race. In keeping with his customary humble style, Owens made no attempt to lambaste the Fuehrer. Strangely, however, it was Franklin Roosevelt whom Jessie believed had snubbed him, when he responded ". . . the President didn't even send me a telegram" and neither was an invitation to the White House forthcoming. Owens, nonetheless, did receive a huge New York City ticker tape parade for his notable achievement, but was later forced to ride in a freight car elevator when attending the dinner in his honor at the esteemed Waldorf Astoria. When incorporating the historical relevance of Jesse Owens and his accomplishments into my lectures, it has always been my observation that students on either end of the racial spectrum find his story both fascinating and remarkable transcending any existing racial divides.

A person of equal historical intrigue, Joe Louis Barrow or the "Brown Bomber" as he was commonly referred to, provides another example of a common man becoming elevated to a higher purpose. Louis likewise came from humble beginnings. He was also born in the Deep South, the grandson of slaves, into a family who similarly joined the mass exodus of blacks heading north for greater social and economic opportunity. Like many African Americans of the era, Louis was raised in the church and assumed a rather shy demeanor. Raised in the Detroit area, young Joe was drawn to the world of boxing, as academic pursuits were probably not within his grasp. Louis' ascension in the boxing realm was remarkable, known for his hard-hitting punch and legendary stamina. As a professional he even "knocked out" the terrifying champion Max Baer (who was believed to be responsible for the death of two previous fighters) and did so in only four rounds ("Franklin & Moss, 2000, p. 476).

Louis' moment in history arrived in two fights with famed German boxer Max Schmeling, who became the poster child for Hitler's theory of Aryan superiority. Schmeling absolutely looked the part, and after intensely studying archival film footage (depicting flaws in Louis' follow through), and after a marathon bout of twelve rounds, Schmeling succeeded in knocking out the 6 foot 2 inch Joe Louis. The entire world was watching, at a time when once again our national pride was being assailed by the alleged master race. And like the stock market crash of 1929, so too did the nation's hopes come crashing down. Louis was devastated, the New York Post wrote that "An idol fell . . . and so totally unexpectedly that it broke the hearts of Negros of the world" ("American Experience," n.d., p. 2). Through a series of back door dealings and ultimately court interventions, Louis was given a second chance for a title fight in 1938, again fighting his old nemesis Max Schmeling. This time Louis was on a mission, hunkered down and secluded in upstate New York, Louis prepared tirelessly, realizing as he put it ". . . the whole damned country was depending on me." ("Joe Louis," n.d.,Louis vs. Schmeling II section, para. 1). Several weeks before the much touted fight, Louis was summoned to the White House where President Roosevelt lamented, "Joe, we need muscles like yours to beat Germany." ("Joe Louis," n.d., Louis vs. Schmeling II section, para. 1). More than a championship title was on the line, the nation's honor was once again at stake. Additional statements made by high-ranking German officials suggesting that a black man could not defeat the German Juggernaut only further inflamed the quiet and introspective Louis.

On June 22, 1938, America and other regions of the globe (including those nations held in bondage or facing imminent threat from fascist forces then threatening to sweep Europe) held their collective breath as the Behemoths of the boxing world stood toe-to-toe in New York's Yankee stadium. More than a boxing match, it was perhaps a clash of cultures, and two distinctly different forces of civilization were both vying to serve as templates for future governmental rule in an increasingly chaotic and fractured global community. In New York City, and much of the nation, taxi cabs parked along the sidewalks, as stores and taverns with their doors drawn open broadcast the momentous event. As Louis himself put it, "I knew I had to get Schmeling good." In little more than two minutes, the German fighter was knocked to the mat several times, precipitating the intervention of the referees, who were then compelled to call the fight. ("Joe Louis," n.d., Louis vs. Schmeling II section, para. 1 & 4) The pride of the nation could scarcely be contained, followed by wild celebrations spilling out into the city streets, and lasting well into the early morning hours. To America it was redress to propounded Aryan superiority, and an affirmation that our institutions, culture, and perhaps even our very civilization itself was not defunct, and that the Third Reich might after all, not be infallible. During the ensuing hostilities of World War II, both Louis and Schmeling would serve in their country's respective armies. Louis solidified his endearing place in the hearts of Americans, both black and white, when he suggested in 1943 that "we are gonna win 'cause we're on God's side" ("Joe Louis," n.d., World War II section, para. 2). Both men survived the war and later went on to become good friends for the balance of their lives. In truth, Schmeling had no particular affinity for Adolf Hitler and his belief in racial superiority. Later in his life, Schmeling even offered to lend money to Joe Louis, who was legendary for his financial mismanagement.

The era of the 1930's was both a disturbing and haunting time in American history, in the wake of international challenges, economic collapse and internal turmoil. The great tyrannical dictators and empires were on the rise, and our treasured and long-standing institutions appeared at times to be inept and increasingly incapable of providing for our sustenance and long-term progress. Strangely, it was two African Americans only generations removed from slavery, and who could not even sit at a lunch counter with their white counterparts, and yet who maintained sufficient faith in the promise of a nation, so as to demonstrate that America in the 1930's may have been supine and on the mat, but most definitely was not out for the count. It may even have been that America's institutions and social structures flawed as they were, still perhaps afforded the best opportunity above and beyond anything the great dictators had to offer, in which to fulfill the future dreams and aspirations of the oppressed and beleaguered, but yet hopeful black masses.

When I first learned of Malcolm X (born Malcolm Little), my reaction must have been commensurate with that of most of white America in the late 1960's. Malcolm's radical views and often corrosive expressions were not in line with the predominant white culture, who often was gainfully employed living in three bedroom suburban ranches in established communities largely steeped in tradition and Christian ideals. As for myself, a member of the cub scouts, little league baseball, and attending an all-white suburban elementary school, those more radical and militant aspects of the black movement somewhat frightened me, and represented a potentially destructive component to my otherwise safe and organized world, and probably represented the same to pervasively white communities all across America. As the late 1960's approached Vietnam protests, racial riots and assassinations began to permeate the American landscape, and that which Malcolm X espoused only represented an additional destabilizing factor in what was already a divisive and tumultuous decade. It wasn't until much later in life that I learned more about this ineffable whirlwind of an activist, as several of my students, upon my request submitted research papers pertaining to this enigmatic man of controversy.

Malcolm Little's biography reads like a Greek tragedy in many respects. Malcolm's father, a Baptist minister and ardent supporter of the Black Nationalist Marcus Garvey, was outspoken and subject to persistent threats and ridicule, therefore, compelling the Little family to relocate frequently. In fact, the family residence in Lansing, Michigan was fire-bombed and ultimately burned to the ground. Only two years later in 1931 Malcolm's father was found, believed to have been murdered, and later abandoned, near a set of railroad tracks, even though authorities found the evidence to be inconclusive. Additionally, four of Malcolm's uncles were similarly found murdered only further adding to the family's history of tragedy. Compounding the difficulties facing the Little family, Malcolm's mother, Louise, suffered a complete emotional breakdown and was committed to a mental institution, after which Malcolm and his brothers and sisters were dispersed to various foster homes and orphanages. Irrespective of these numerous disadvantages, Malcolm somehow managed to graduate from Junior High School among the top students of his class. In high school Malcolm was dissuaded from pursuing studies towards a potential career in law, when a teacher suggested that pursuing law would be an unattainable aspiration and "no realistic goal for a nigger."

After dropping out from high school (a pattern all too familiar with today's black youth), Malcolm vacillated between Boston, Massachusetts and Harlem, New York, where he began to assume the guiles of a street smart and petty criminal, earning the nick name of "Detroit Red." Participating in small burglaries and break-ins and the occasional selling of illicit drugs (not to mention gambling and prostitution), Malcolm was eventually arrested and incarcerated, ultimately being sentenced to a period of ten years, but only serving seven due to good behavior. Using his time in prison judiciously, Malcolm set about furthering his studies in history, religion, and philosophy, even concentrating heavily on the dictionary in order to extend his vocabulary. But, it was in prison that Malcolm was exposed to the teachings of Islam by his brother Reginald, who skewed him into the direction of the Lost-Found Nation of Islam under the direction of Elijah Muhammad. It was here that Malcolm was taught that the white race was evil and doomed to destruction by Allah, and that the best course of action was for blacks to disassociate themselves altogether from western white civilization in all respects including religion, philosophy, politics and culture. Practicing his new religion faithfully, Malcolm even abstained from drinking, smoking and the consuming of pork, as many Muslims do, but now adding to his life the additional elements of structure and discipline.

Upon his release from prison Malcolm made his way to the Chicago area to meet and then to ultimately study under the renowned Elijah Muhammad, where he was given the name Malcolm X in order to shun his supposed "slave name" of Little. Then shortly thereafter Malcolm was dispatched to help organize additional mosques in both the Philadelphia and Harlem regions. In part because of his innate intelligence and his familiarity with the written word, Malcolm X was summoned to become a national spokesman for the black Muslims in order to help expand their influence and message. At a time when America was beginning to address matters of race and attempting to bridge racial divides through programs of integration and civil rights legislation, Malcolm X, and the black Muslims were strongly advocating racial segregation, even calling for blacks to take self-defensive measures in the face of alleged white violence. Moreover, Malcolm X believed that civil rights legislation and the passive resistance measures being taken early on by the reverend Dr. Martin Luther King and others would not bring about redress or equality among the races. Malcolm X, who was making the rounds of the TV talk show and radio circuit, further inflamed the white masses and even many blacks, when referring to the November 1963 assassination of President Kennedy, as a case of "the chickens coming home to roost." This proved too much even for Elijah Muhammad, who was already having personal issues with the sometimes abrasive Malcolm X. Elijah Muhammad opted to place him on an imposed verbal suspension for a period of 90 days. Believing to have been slighted, Malcolm severed his connections with the Nation of Islam, announcing that he intended to pursue the creation of two additional Islamic activist organizations, the Muslim Mosque Inc. and the Organization of Afro-American Unity.

Further incendiary commentary was found when Malcolm advised African Americans not to participate in the voting processes, which to that point had been a primary focal point of the civil rights movement. He continued to call for the abandonment of non-violent methods in which to achieve equality, even suggesting that the high crime rates so prevalent in black communities was a direct result of following lifestyle patterns of the prevailing white community. Perhaps most offensive of all, was Malcolm's call for black people to relinquish their attachment to the Christian faith, which he believed to be a white man's religion.

However, Malcolm's tone did begin to soften after he made a personal pilgrimage to the holy city of Mecca in Saudi Arabia in 1964. While pleading his case to Middle Eastern, European and African venues, Malcolm X found sympathetic audiences and began to perceive matters of race in a more broad, general and international context. He said he no longer viewed all white people as inherently evil, and believed that through his pilgrimage, he had found the true meaning of the Islamic faith. Additionally, he stated that while traveling overseas he had met blond haired, blue eyed men I could call my brothers. (Colorado State University, n.d., The Oneness of Man Under One God section, para. 4-5).

Malcolm now believed he had a message for all races, and upon his return to the U.S., even began to advocate for mutual cooperation between black and white communities on all levels, including voter registration, public schools, and various institutional levels of law enforcement and other governmental agencies. These new and more subtle attitudes manifested much to the displeasure of the Nation of Islam, who it was believed, in part due to Malcolm's ongoing feud with organization head Elijah Muhammad, was determined to eradicate the outspoken activist. In February of 1965 Malcolm's home was once again fire-bombed and he, his wife and children escaped serious injury. However, even after seeking the added insurance of body guards, only weeks later, Malcolm X's adversaries succeeded in gunning down the 39-year-old social activist while speaking in a Manhattan ball room. Malcolm was survived by his pregnant wife and six children (a set of twins were born shortly after his assassination) and his legacy continues to resonate to this day.

Malcolm X, it seems to me, represents that which the white community perhaps fears most, change of the existing status quo and the potential to use violent means, if necessary, to affect that change. But given his violent heritage and upbringing in a hostile white environment, who could fault Malcolm for his extremist tendencies in order to attain his life-long quest and vigorous pursuit for the ever allusive goal of social justice? As for myself, being unaware of Malcolm's circumstances, in part, made me ignorant of who the man truly was, and what he came to represent. In many ways to me this is illustrative of the Cold War environment in which I was raised. From the time I was a child in elementary school, I was instructed to hide under desks and to seek protection in fall out shelters in anticipation of the Soviet attack many believed to be imminent. "Better dead than red" was the mantra of the 1950's and 60's and nightly we went to bed, sometimes prayed, and generally feared the ultimate confrontation we were certain would one day transpire. It was, in part, out of this fear that later I decided to pursue history so as to be able to better understand our potential opponents and the forces which have shaped the world around us. Using this acquired knowledge I then intended to work in the intelligence community or possibly even the Armed Forces in order to make a positive contribution in preserving and maintaining our system of government, culture and ultimately our way of life. But as it turns out I became an educator and as a professor teaching Polish and Russian students after the precipitous collapse of the Soviet Union, where I trod on the grounds of my supposed childhood nemesis. Photographing Soviet Mig fighters, having my picture taken in front of statues of Lenin, and then ultimately being invited into the private homes of Russian and Polish families, I came to understand these were not the "boogie men" that I had been taught to hate and to fear. It wasn't these more Central and Eastern European persons we needed to fear, but rather it was their oppressive governments, and their sometimes dark and hidden agendas. Similarly, while examining the historical contribution of individuals like Malcolm X, Paul Robeson, Jessie Owens, and Joe Louis, and welcoming African Americans into my home, and finally both learning and instructing their history, I came to have an understanding of where the black culture stands and where it has come from, thus mitigating my own apprehensions of what the black community is attempting to achieve, and where it is intending to go.

Even in my present lectures to predominantly white students, the recounting of these events and contributions made by these remarkable and resilient African Americans, continues to transcend racial lines and resonate as a universal source of American historical pride. In my estimation the preceding accounts of individual African American achievement exemplifies the contribution made to the overall development of our national character. And while every American school child is today familiar with the accomplishments of great black Americans such as Dr. Martin Luther King and Harriet Tubman, it would be, beneficent and moreover productive, if the cadre of these aforementioned African Americans (such as Booker T. Washington, W.E.B. DuBois, Paul Robeson, Joe Louis or even Jesse Owens), could be incorporated into public school curriculums, thus fostering greater understanding and mutual appreciation across America's broad and diverse cultural spectrum.

CHAPTER VI

Blacks in Arms

IN ALL MANNERS pertaining to the African American experience and its long progressive march towards equality, few seem to promote greater pride within the black race itself than the contributions made to America's colorful military heritage. In our nation's panorama of conflict, African Americans have stood shoulder-to-shoulder with their white brethren from Bunker Hill to the battle of Baghdad. This National service historically has served as a common thread inextricably linking the two races throughout their sometimes contentious history of coexistence. The only American conflict found not to contain elements of blacks-in-arms was the Mexican-American War (1846-48), in which the United States government deliberately excluded them. African Americans have sought to utilize this more combative avenue, as a means to promote their own social agenda for justice and advancement, through commitment, personal courage, and a willingness to subject themselves to potential physical harm, if necessary, for the cause of a greater purpose (Edgerton, 2001, p. 5). It is interesting to note, that in times of military emergency or national crisis, the issue or significance of discrimination seems to diminish, seeming to ebb and flow with the fortunes and tides of war. The roots of discrimination were deep and well-entrenched and can be found to predate even the American Revolution. However, African Americans stayed the course, leaving an endearing legacy of contribution and one of invaluable national service.

The following accounts offer both graphic and poignant depictions of that commitment at a juncture when African American citizenship was either unacknowledged or regarded as secondary at best.

On the eve of the American Revolution, British colonies, even those in the South such as the Carolinas and Virginia, sought black military service as a means to augment their meager volunteer colonial militias, in order to combat French and Spanish encroachment and even native American interference. During the French and Indian War (1754-1763), in the sometimes guerilla-oriented and murderous affair for control of the North American continent between the premier powers of Europe and their colonial constituents, black troops were solicited with regularity as a means of securing additional military advantage or leverage. After a successful execution of that war, however, the British colonies, in part, due to their pervasive fear of blacks or slaves in arms, sought both to diminish the role of African Americans as "naturally cowardly," and then as a matter of policy, began to prohibit or discourage future African American military service through legislative processes, citing "there must be great caution used, lest our slaves, when arm'd, become our masters" (Edgerton, 2001, p. 7).

One of the key players in an event commonly referred to as "The Boston Massacre" was in fact himself a free black dock worker, named Crispus Attuks. By all accounts Crispus was a bit of an intransigent and brawler, and often was found to be in proximity to that city's numerous bars and taverns. Early in the evening on March 5, 1770, Attuks and others who probably were aided by various libations, encountered a small contingent of British forces then occupying that city as part of an external police force, designed in part to punish the city of Boston for its revolutionary conduct. Initially words and insults were hurled between the two forces with Attuks at the forefront, and then followed by the hurling of snow balls and ice with some of those possibly being mixed with stones. The small British contingent increasingly isolated and overwhelmed by the growing and angry crowd, and, with their backs to the proverbial wall, responded in consequence by firing into the mob. Crispus was one of the first to fall (along with four other Bostonians), and as such emerges as one of America's first martyrs, making his role in the affair, and in our nation's history as one of irony and yet, one of prominence.

The American Revolution (1775-81) presented enormous challenges for a race largely held in bondage and who had little stake in the affair, and yet was simultaneously being pulled in two directions by the primary combatants. In this war for American Independence, which ensued (in part due to the Boston massacre), General Washington was found to have "Negros" in the hastily composed Continental army, which was made up of a collection of New Englanders, Southerners, and those associated with the mid-Atlantic colonies. New Englanders at times harbored free-blacks, who remained as an inflammatory affront to those regiments from the South. After the battle of Bunker or Breeds Hill, and after feeling some measure of initial success, Washington was compelled to issue an order stating, "Negros, boys unable to bear neither arms, nor old men were to be further enlisted" (McCullough, 2005, p. 120). However, later on in 1776, when his fortunes began to reverse and the American cause of revolution appeared near imminent collapse, Washington was compelled to rescind that order. Part of the reason for Washington's reversal, was the issuance by the British governor of Virginia, Lord Dunsmore and his famous proclamation of November 1777, offering freedom to any slave who could somehow extricate himself from control of their colonial masters (Norton, Katzman, Escott, Chudacoff, 1998, p. 152). In the end only some 2,000 blacks actually saw service in the king's army, but its real task was designed to disrupt colonial commerce, and to invite potential slave revolts. Of the 2,000 blacks that served, nearly half died of a small pox epidemic and the rest were relatively inconsequential in the attempt to tip the scales of war. As for Washington's beleaguered continental army, blacks again were allowed to enter the ranks, but most were already free blacks. One of Washington's Lieutenants, General John Thomas, and commander of Massachusetts units stated ". . . we have some Negros, but I look upon them in general equally serviceable with other men, for fatigue and in action, many of them have proved themselves brave" (McCullough, 2005, p. 36).

An African American too was to be found in the nationally renowned Lewis & Clark Expedition (1804 to 1806) and among its esteemed members of the elite "Corps of Discovery" as it was then known. By today's standards, the expedition had the hallmark signs of a modern day CIA operation. Authorized by President Jefferson in 1804, the Captains set out to document the American West, in anticipation of a possible American coup to secure the region then belonging to the French Emperor Napoleon (Ambrose, 1996, p. 76).

Captain Clark insisted upon bringing his personal slave, York, who was, in truth, more of a life-long friend and companion. Even though the initial cadre of the corps was only anticipated to be comprised of twelve men, mostly of military composition, Clark believed York, an athletic, agile man of immense physical stature, would prove indispensable to the operation and its success. York was a man of deep and dark complexion, and when the party encountered numerous Indian tribes and villages on their protracted journey, natives were fascinated by his extreme color, even at times attempting to determine if it could in fact be washed off. References are to be found in the journals of both Lewis and Clark, to that of York, because of his sustenance and girth, who was on more than one occasion observed chasing Indian children in mock games of "Monster" and "hide-and-seek," whereby children's screams and laughter often manifested, and whose net affect was to facilitate more relaxed relations between the corps of discovery and their sometimes apprehensive native hosts. In the end, York's sheer physical prowess did indeed prove to be at least beneficial, if not altogether indispensable to the rigorous and often stringent execution of the Expedition, which laid the groundwork for America's ultimate westward expansion.

The War of 1812 perhaps saw a more mitigated role for African Americans in this, our second great struggle with the British Empire, as Congress authorized the raising of two regiments of "men of color," consisting of only a thousand men each (Franklin & Moss, 2000, p. 123). However, in the most famous confrontation of that war, the battle of New Orleans (actually fought after a formal cessation of hostilities); blacks were found to be on the front lines. The war itself, a collection of small battles and skirmishes, came to a crescendo in January 1815, when a collection of forces, then under the command of Major General Andrew Jackson, were thrown together to resist a possible British invasion of the city of New Orleans. Success there might mean possibly gaining control of the mouth of the Mississippi, and then ultimately that of the river itself. Jackson's contingents were formed of American regulars, Tennessee and Kentucky volunteers (with their notorious long rifles), Indians, citizens of the city including companies of free African American units, and a cadre of pirates associated with the infamous Jean Lafitte. They were aligned in built-up defensive positions constructed of cotton, timber and various other materials to thwart a British force of some 6,000 under British Commander Pakenham. These were battle-hardened British regulars, who fully anticipated pushing aside the ad hoc collection of Americans. To the British, eyeing the numerous factions of the continental defenders, it must have seemed to them like the circus was in town. Jackson's "circus," however, held its fortified position against two separate British assaults, inflicting up to what at that time was Britain's worst military defeat, as over 2,000 British casualties succumbed to American long rifles and artillery. The Americans suffered only 21 casualties. It has been largely ascribed that due in part to the victory at New Orleans, where African Americans were present, that America may have bested the British.

Of all the conflicts in which African American forces were operative or present, few approach in magnitude and scope, that of the American Civil War, and particularly the exploits of the 54th Massachusetts all-volunteer African American regiment under the command of a cadre of white officers, and the indomitable Colonel Robert Gould Shaw. In the great contest of 1861-1865, African Americans were initially non-combatants, but as the conflict escalated into what ultimately became a war of attrition, blacks and former slaves began to figure prominently into the overall equation. What was supposed to be a "white man's war" quickly mutated into a multifaceted and multiracial conflict. Governor John Andrews of Massachusetts was one of the early proponents calling for the creation of Negro units to aid the Union in its execution of the war. Assisted in his efforts by the stoic Frederick Douglass who quipped "once let the black man get upon his person the brass letters, "U.S."; let him get an eagle on his button, and a musket on his shoulder and bullets in his pocket, and there is no power on earth which can deny that he has earned the right to `citizenship' in the United States" (Cox, 1991, p. 3).

The 54th Massachusetts was created in part out of the desires of Governor Andrew. Colonel Shaw (wounded previously at the Battle of Antietam) was chosen because of his family's more progressive views and previous relations with the Governor. Shaw was determined that through hard work and discipline, his black regiment would be placed in combat so as to serve as a model, which future black forces could emulate, and begin to earn their place in what was surely to be a new social order upon a Union victory. In truth, however, most Union commanders had no such intentions, as black units were thought to be designated for subsidiary roles such as supply, engineering and even the digging of latrines. Moreover, the idea of blacks in arms was a frightening prospect to a nation still grappling with the concept of the Emancipation Proclamation itself, and the freeing of the black race as a whole. Shaw and his troops were made to suffer immense indignation and humiliation time and time again. Uniforms were deliberately late in arriving; pay from the quartermaster was reduced in half, all in an attempt to reinforce the social biases of the day. Regarding the issue of reduced pay for black soldiers, a common assertion of the period was that "Uncle Abe" had gotten himself a real bargain, as a black man was every bit as capable of stopping a bullet, as was a white man, and for half the price. While completing their initial program of training, Shaw's 54th and their white officers were read the Confederate States of America Proclamation, citing that any black soldier captured in arms would be returned to the condition of slavery, and similarly any white officer leading said troops would be held accountable as inciting servile revolution and as such would be subject to execution (Franklin & Moss, 2000, p. 240-241). Ultimately the 54th and other black units were sent into fields of operation and points south, but largely in supportive and non-combat roles. Through Shaw's insistence, and letters to Governor Andrew and the Lincoln administration, his 54th was transferred into fields of operation and were no longer required to face the indignity of digging latrines, or the inglorious duty of incessant foraging operations.

In all some 200,000 blacks, free or otherwise, would join the Union cause in the Navy, Artillery, Calvary, but most would be assigned to Infantry units where they very much aspired to those ideals espoused by the great Frederick Douglass. In nearly 450 engagements and 39 major battles, black forces indeed did distinguish themselves with nearly 38,000 African Americans making the supreme sacrifice (a 40% mortality rate higher than white troops) and 16 winning the nation's highest honor as Congressional Medal of Honor recipients (Franklin & Moss, 2000, p. 243). In a similar vein, even Confederate authorities came to appreciate the intrinsic value of blacks-in-arms when, in early 1865, Jefferson Davis with the concurrence of Robert E. Lee, attempted to implement similar plans offering slaves the potential of freedom if they agreed to take up Confederate arms. Affected earlier, the plan may have yielded some results, but by April of that same year the matter was finally concluded at Appomattox Court House, Virginia.

The 54th went on to distinguish itself most namely at Olustee, Honey Hill and its infamous frontal assault of the impregnable Fort Wagner. Most military strategists regarded the well-fortified Charleston Fort with its casement sand bunkers and surrounding marshes and extraordinarily tough nut to crack, if it could even be taken at all. In July of 1864, the Union scheduled an artillery barrage by sea to be followed from land by a massive frontal assault of the Confederate fort. Colonel Shaw, seeing an opportunity and knowing newspaper and magazine coverage would be extensive, volunteered the services of his gallant 54th to lead the frontal assault and to showcase its capabilities. Moving into position, the Massachusetts unit was cheered by fellow Union soldiers, white and black alike, for what appeared to many to be a task in futility. At low tide, the 54th advanced under an artillery attack from nearby Fort Sumter (still in Confederate hands) with Shaw gallantly waving his sword. However, after being sufficiently pinned down, the Colonel ordered his black troops to hunker down in the sand dunes, and to prepare for a fixed bayonet charge to be judiciously effected under the cover of darkness. After nightfall the contest continued with vigor as the 54th, led by Shaw, scrambled upwards in the face of the most intense artillery, musket and grenade fire. From Union observers in the distance, pitiful cries and intense flashes could be both heard and seen, and at one point the stars and stripes appeared on the Forts parapets. Confederate and black alike fought like madmen in utter hand-to-hand combat. Colonel Shaw was killed approaching the Fort (shot through the chest), but his death only angered and further inspired the 54th to fight. Passing over the ramparts, cresting over the Fort, the Massachusetts black troops appeared to be on the precipice of victory. Morning light, however, revealed images of dark grotesque figures washing upon the shore, bodies strewn everywhere throughout the sand. The Confederate bars and stripes still flew over the fort. Even the 54th could not pull off the impossible, but its heroic frontal assault would go down in the annals of military history as perhaps one of the most inspiring, gripping and heroic of all times. The Massachusetts 54th colored regiment would be known forever thereafter as the "Glory regiment" with company "C's" Sergeant Carney winning the Congressional Medal of Honor. Some of the captured 54th were arrested and sent to the city of Charleston, and were threatened with execution (Cox, 1991, p. 103). Colonel Shaw was, in a gesture of indignity, stripped of his clothes and buried in a mass grave with his black troops in front of the fort, with the rebel commander vehemently touting, "We have buried him with his Niggers." On that July evening of 1864 African American dues into the brotherhood of Americans in Arms were paid in full measure. Moreover, the question of whether blacks were equal to the task of service, battle, fortitude and courage would henceforth be resolved.

Nearly 35 years after the Emancipation Proclamation itself was issued, war again would illuminate the extent of America's racial divide, as the Spanish American war of 1898 provided the first test whereby all Americans, Northerners and Southerners, whites and blacks, as a collective nation would engage enemy combatants. This conflict sometimes referred to as the "Splendid Little War" would not be fought on the scale of the American Civil War, but again the mettle of black forces would be tested. The explosion of the battleship, the USS Maine, on February 15th, is ascribed as the event which precipitated the war. The explosion took the lives of 250 officers and enlisted men, 22 of whom were black, which meant that blacks had a personal stake in the affair (Franklin & Moss, 2000, p. 329). Moreover, many African Americans signed up as volunteers eager to join the fight in the cause to free primarily black Cubans, whom they believed were oppressed by their white Spanish masters. A handful of Infantry regiments and several cavalry units stationed in western Indian Territory, (sometimes called Buffalo soldiers) already existed, but Congress authorized the establishment of nine additional black outfits to be created and pressed into service, as part of an overall request for an additional 200,000 volunteers to supplement standing American forces. The stipulation for black forces in arms was that as a general rule blacks were to be commissioned as officers no higher in rank than that of 2nd Lieutenant, so as not to inflame white troops operating in similar theatres of operation. In 1898, blacks were still thought to be ill-suited for active roles in leadership, and of command structure.

During the conflict and in all theatres of operation from Cuba to the Philippines, black soldiers performed well. Black troops showed what they were made of even during the much celebrated charge of the rough riders (a collection of cowboys, Indians, college students and blacks) under the command of Colonel of Volunteer Theodore Roosevelt and their subsequent audacious frontal assault of San Juan Hill on June the 24th. Elements of that charge were composed of units of the black 10th cavalry which fought that day along with white units of the first volunteer cavalry. By all accounts the black 10th cavalry played a pivotal role in the illustrious charge. According to Lieutenant Thomas Roberts, himself a participant that day, "I have naught but the highest praise for the swarthy warriors on the field of carnage. Led by brave men, they will go into the thickest of fight, even to the wicked mouths of deadly cannon, unflinchingly . . ." (Franklin & Moss, 2000, p. 332). One white soldier of the rough riders exclaimed, "Well, the ninth and tenth men are alright, they can drink out of our canteens."

But all was not forgiven during the short lived conflict; elements of Jim Crow continued. During one heated exchange between U.S. Infantry forces and the Spanish who held the high ground, and with assistance from artillery units, the Spanish succeeded in forcing the Americans to take cover under a small cliff outcropping. Spanish sniper fire pinned down the American troops under this cramped but protective natural umbrella. However, as additional U.S. troops sought this protective outcropping, space became a premium and subsequently black units were made to leave its protective cover in favor of successive white units, later seeking the same refuge, resulting in a number of casualties among the "Smoked Yankees" as the Spanish were prone to call the black troops (Franklin & Moss, 2000, p. 333). Later on even Theodore Roosevelt was found to back-peddle, when in an article he alleged that black troops performed well enough when under the leadership of white officers, but that during the famous charge up San Juan hill black forces nearly retreated until he himself with revolver in hand intervened and personally stemmed the retreating black tide. Nonetheless, blacks had once again stepped up to the plate and performed their civic duties, serving with honor and distinction in America's first multi-racial conflict in arms. Winning at least four Congressional medals of Honor and serving with Northerners and Southerners alike, African Americans were still forced, however, to serve under the constraints of segregation and Jim Crow. Irrespective, blacks could reflect upon their role with pride.

At the dawn of the twentieth century the African American community would face new and daunting challenges culminating in the "Great War" (1914-1918), which would later be reconfigured and forever known as World War I. America's role in that conflict did not reach a crescendo until 1917, which can be largely attributed to Germany's unrestricted submarine warfare, emanating in the sinking of the Lusitania in May of 1915 (resulting in the loss of nearly 1,200 souls) as well as the Zimmerman telegram, whereby Germany promised to return the territories of Texas, Colorado, California, Arizona, etc. in exchange for a guaranteed Mexican alliance should armed conflict with America arise. Given the pervasive racial climate, many African Americans were reluctant to offer their wholesale political or military support. Despite President Woodrow Wilson's campaign slogan for a second term, ("Vote for Wilson he kept us out of war.") the President in April of 1917 asked Congress for a formal declaration of war against the forces of Germany, Austria-Hungary and the central powers of Europe. The following May a selective service program was implemented, and an army of nearly five million was raised, trained, with approximately two million being sent into active service in France under the guise of the American Expedition

Force. Of the nearly five-million-man U.S. Force, just fewer than 500,000 were of African American decent, all being sent in theory, if not in practice, to help "keep the world safe for democracy."

For many in the black community including W.E.B. Du Bois, this placed African Americans in a conundrum which could not be easily reconciled. How blacks could be morally obliged to fight for democracy overseas when in fact most of those espoused "democratic ideals" could not often be found in black communities' right here in America. Moreover, many Southerners were again reluctant to place blacks under arms, unless they were relegated to strictly support and supply duties, and then once again placed into segregated units with white command structures. Du Bois (who later accepted a captains' commission) supported the idea of segregated black officer training facilities as a means to "take advantage of the disadvantage." According to Du Bois, "we (blacks) must choose then between the insult of a separate camp and the irreparable injury of strengthening the present custom of putting no black men in positions of authority" (Norton et al., 2001, p. 642-643).[1] In the end, collegiate institutes such as Hampton and Fisk University promoted the idea, and subsequently more than fourteen hundred black officers would join the ranks of the American Expeditionary Force.

Training camps for both black and white recruits were scattered mostly throughout the Northeast and in Southern portions of the country. Primarily due to logistical and economic reasons. But the South remained opposed to the idea of black units being trained within its jurisdictions. The War Department, however, largely upheld the necessity of Southern training facilities, and resentment continued to grow among white Southerners, with the fear of blacks-in-arms still resonating nearly as strong as it did in the late 1860's. Hostilities between black recruits and white locals began to spread throughout the South in 1917 (Franklin & Moss, 2000, p. 365). The situation peaked in August that same year, when blacks of the 24th Infantry came into direct conflict with local white citizens of nearby Houston, Texas. After authorities attempted to disarm the unit, blacks, who feared the weapons would then be turned against them, responded in consequence, thereby killing seventeen whites. When order was finally restored, thirteen members of the black 24th were sentenced to death in what can only be regarded as a sham of a trial and with

---

[1] Interesting to note some fifteen thousand Native Americans served in the U.S. Armed Forces, but they however were not segregated.

an additional forty-one of those black troops being sentenced to life imprisonment. In most instances the federal government sought to train these troops as rapidly as possible, and then to expedite their movements to Europe (France in particular), where many would be integrated into French forces already bogged down in a stalemate facing German forces north and east of Paris.

Upon arrival in France, many African American units were assigned the task of supply, provision and engineering and into Stevedore battalions, whose primary task was to prepare for the anticipated influx of U.S. troops to that region. Some black units including the 93rd division, the 369th and the 370th U.S. infantry, however, were designed for combat purposes, being then further trained by French authorities to augment their weakened divisions, many of whom were suffering staggering losses and from sagging morale.

By all accounts African American units performed remarkably well under French military command and structure. After being acquainted with the atrocities of total war and the "meat grinder affect" of the technology of twentieth century warfare, blacks began to win the admiration and respect of French forces and citizens alike. The French community and culture afforded African Americans great respect, freedom and latitude, even extending their black comrades-in-arms personal invitations into their private homes. All of this much to the chagrin of whites of the American Expeditionary Force, who attempted to discredit their black brethren in arms by suggesting to French officials that blacks were sexually voracious, and often harbored criminal tendencies, which was precisely why social institutions such as segregation and Jim Crow had to be implemented and enforced in American society (Franklin & Moss, 2000, p. 372). In the end, the French, however, largely ignored these stigmas even awarding African American units some of their nation's highest honors including the Distinguished Service Cross, Distinguished Service Medal, and the esteemed Croix deGuerre.

Of those black forces, operating entirely under American command, and led by the venerable General "Jack" Pershing, most were integrated into the Infantry, Navy, and National Guard units. However, legislation prohibited them from participating within the U.S. Marines and the recently established U.S. Air Corps. Again, within these divisions African American service remained indispensable as those troops saw action from Champagne to St. Mihel, and from the Argonne Forrest to the occupation of the Rhine. And while even "Jack" Pershing cited certain blacks for gallantry and bravery, not one black soldier of the great conflict, was to become the recipient of our nations highest honor, the Congressional Medal of Honor. Only posthumously did Corporal Freddie Stowers of Sandy Spring, South Carolina receive the award in 1991 when it was bestowed upon him by President Bush to his elderly surviving sisters, in an attempt to right this most egregious infliction of U.S. History (Franklin & Moss, 2000, p. 368).

Again as in previous times of military peril, black forces willingly participated, while simultaneously attempting to advance their cause for social justice. For most African American soldiers returning from European theatres of operation, they were eager to return to both America and their loved ones. For some, however, they were reticent if not altogether reluctant to return to a pervasively racist American society, especially in light of the relative equality and justice displayed by their French hosts. Moreover, despite the warm reception in 1919 of parades and banners upon their subsequent return (even Buffalo held a truly remarkable reception), most would be exposed to the enormous forces of latent hostility, and still returning as a segregated fighting force subject to overt discrimination, racial riots and an ever-changing American social landscape.

Similar patterns again would surface on the precipice of World War II regarding the races, and their respective military service to the nation. Emerging from the throws of the great depression, America's standing army was less than one quarter of a million strong (Americas military might was ranked as only 21st on a global scale), of which less than five thousand of those were of African American decent. When, in an attempt to prepare for impending hostilities with the Third Reich, or possibly even the empire of Japan, the U.S., implemented a selective service act in 1940 in order to draw in perspective recruits. In precedence setting fashion, local draft boards often actively discriminated against blacks, soliciting primarily white recruits. While America had become the great arsenal for democracy, many blacks could not even find work in the expanding defense industries and therefore, sought orientation into the nation's armed forces.

On the eve of the second Great War against the forces of tyranny, some progress at home regarding matters of race was being advanced. Colonel B. O. Davis, the highest ranking African American in the U.S. Armed Forces, was elevated to the rank of brigadier general (a move many believed to be nothing more than a reelection ploy by the Roosevelt administration) destroying that last restrictive ceiling of rank. But still the fact remained; America's Armed Forces remained as segregated as they had existed from the time of the Civil War. In July of 1940, black organizations including the National Youth Administration and the N.A.A.C.P., began to organize a proposed massive march on Washington, D.C., in order to demand more corrective government action, and to again level the playing field. Such a march would have been a most embarrassing public relations opportunity for opponents of a nation beginning to marshal its forces to fight those countries alleging Aryan and Japanese racial superiority. Due in part to the negotiations of the President's wife, Mrs. Eleanor Roosevelt (in whom the black race would find an avenging angel), the potentially embarrassing march of protest was avoided when the administration issued its famous Executive Order Number 8802, prohibiting the discrimination of minorities in industry or labor organizations (Franklin & Moss, 2000, p.480).

During World War II, and the second great global conflict (1941-45) against the forces of tyranny in which approximately one million African Americans served, discrimination and its practices remained the norm, but unprecedented access was afforded to numerous factions within those forces, ranging from the Marine Corps to the Medical Corps, and from Tank Battalions to the Air Service. Even African American women were allowed to serve in a reserve capacity through the Women's Army Corps, and other various extensions (Franklin & Moss, 2000, p. 482). Moreover, for the first time, both white and black officer candidates attended and graduated from the same facilities or officer candidate schools. America's abrupt entry into the world conflict, precipitated by Japans sneak attack of December 7, 1941 at the Pacific base of Pearl Harbor produced an early and unlikely hero in the form of black seamen, Dorie Miller. Miller became the first African American hero of that conflict for his service in manning a machine gun in the face of insurmountable odds against the immense Japanese air attack. For his efforts, Miller (a ship's cook) was awarded the distinguished Navy Cross for his heroic actions on that day. In all, some 500,000 African Americans saw service overseas, performing a wide array of duties, ranging from supply to combat (Franklin & Moss, 2000, p. 483). In the European theatre, black units distinguished themselves from D-Day, fighting their way through France and across the Rhine into Germany. One of those elements, the 761st Tank Battalion, was singled out for its "gallant service" in half a dozen European countries including its indispensable actions in the Battle of the Bulge (Hitler's famous spearheaded attempt to drive the allies into the sea), but was not awarded the illustrious Presidential Distinguished Unit Citation until the 1970's, when it was presented by then President Jimmy Carter (Franklin & Moss, 2000, p. 484-485).

Black integration into the Mediterranean and Pacific theatre of operations was less pervasive and even less illustrious perhaps than in Europe but, nonetheless, those units performed well under extreme conditions and in combat situations. One group, the 92nd division attached to the U.S. 5th army received some criticism for a series of reversals as American forces slugged their way up the Italian peninsula. The Germans who had taken over combat operations from their Italian comrades, fought a dogged retreat often deeply entrenched, requiring the American troops to pay dearly for every mile and every recaptured village. This division had perhaps one of the lowest literacy rates in the army, and may have been poorly officered but, nonetheless, managed to win in excess of 12,000 decorations and citations. African Americans too, saw service in the Pacific and Orient as black troop's filled combat and support roles from the Philippines to the Solomons. Admittedly, many of those roles revolved around construction and provision duties, but many were also simultaneously expected to take up arms while performing those less than memorable but highly relevant tasks. Many of those units, including the 24th combat infantry (who fought the Japanese for control of the new Georgia islands), fought with determination against the most unfavorable of conditions and circumstances, and whose services were nonetheless deemed "steady and consistent" (Franklin & Moss, 2000, p. 486).

For the first time in the history of armed conflict, African Americans actively participated in air combat missions and sorties. The new U.S. Air force as it came to be known, formerly of the U.S. Army Air Corps, was compelled to augment its numbers, creating the black 332nd and the 99th that flew support, escort, and attack operations in both Europe and the Mediterranean. Later a black bombardier group, the 477th was formed, but was activated too late in the war to perform actual bombing operations. From the Tuskegee airmen to the more than 80 African American aviators who became recipients of the distinguished flying cross award, blacks took immense pride in the accomplishments of these determined airmen who in their conscientious achievement and resolve, succeeded in breaking down racial barriers, and in proving that for black Americans, the sky was indeed the limit.

In naval operations, blacks too made inroads into a service that many believed to already be perhaps less racially biased than other elements of America's Armed Forces. Blacks once again served with distinction in various capacities, from the U.S. Navy itself, to the merchant marine fleet, which boasted nearly 25,000 African American personnel who manned those vessels. An estimated 12,500 black fighting Seabees augmented naval forces, as well as additional black marines who protected various bases and military installations. Four black captains commanded U.S. liberty ships comprised of integrated black and white personnel. Nearly twenty U.S. Naval and merchant marine vessels were named after African Americans of notoriety, including the "Booker T. Washington," the "S.S. Harriet Tubman," and the "S.S. Frederick Douglass," which later sank in hostile operations.

Due in part to prodding by the Roosevelt administration (and probably of Mrs. Roosevelt herself), it was announced in January of 1945 that a unit was to be comprised of whites and African Americans and its intended establishment for active duty and service on German soil. The unit was still to be segregated by regiments, but one in which platoons would act in unison during combat operations. Nonetheless, this was a step in the right direction. At the conclusion of hostilities in Europe in April and May of 1945, the U.S. War Department concluded about this integrated unit, and about the black infantry men in particular that they "established themselves as fighting men no less courageous or aggressive than their white comrades" (Franklin & Moss, 2000, p. 485).

During the global conflagration many glass ceilings had indeed been destroyed and blacks as a general rule had made significant headway. African Americans were proud of this service and contribution to the nation, but many wondered if again they had become victims of discrimination. Not since the Spanish American War of 1898 had black troops been awarded the coveted Congressional Medal of Honor, our Nation's highest military award. It took until the late 1990's before a commission was appointed to investigate this apparent historical anomaly, concluding that it was no less than a conspired plan of "racism" to deny those deserving heroes of their just rewards of service. Finally, in January of 1997, six African Americans were awarded the Congressional Medal of Honor posthumously, and a seventh (Vernon Baker) still living saw justice come to fruition.

To be sure, racism as an inherent fixture was still to be found in the U.S. Armed Forces of World War II. But increasingly, America found itself asking the question, "What would Berlin say?" As such, racism became an albatross around the neck of a nation allegedly leading the universal charge against the forces of global tyranny, while simultaneously oppressing minority elements at home. Nonetheless, progress, albeit slow, was progress. And thanks largely or at least in part to the Roosevelt administration, and in particular the seemingly tireless efforts of the First Lady, Eleanor, the African American community in arms could point to achievement, accomplishment and resonant pride in its ascribed role in the twentieth century's greatest conflict, and thus claim "victory at home, and victory abroad" (Franklin & Moss, 2000, p. 488).

The Korean conflict of 1950, only further magnified the advances made during World War II, by blacks in arms, as the U.S. found itself in an ever-widening Asian land campaign, and in a most distinctly numerically disadvantageous situation particularly on the ground. Prior to the conflict, the Truman administration had already taken steps to bring equality to America's Armed Forces and its institutions. Beginning in 1946, committees were appointed by the Executive to investigate matters of racial inequality then existing within America's Armed Forces. In 1949, the army adopted an official policy of opening all positions relative to personnel to all persons regardless of race or color, thus abolishing previous restrictive quota programs which ultimately became a precursor to what was later known as Truman's Fair Deal Policies. When General Matthew Ridgway assumed command of all U.S. forces in the Far East, he immediately solicited the U.S. Department of Defense for its assistance in helping to integrate blacks, and to incorporate them into mainstream U.S. and United Nations forces, then attempting to halt communist forces threatening to overrun the Korean peninsula (Franklin & Moss, 2000, p. 507). Once more in what has been officially labeled as a "Police Action," African Americans again distinguished themselves and won the approval, or at least relative acceptance of their white counterparts and in the most extreme elements of geography and climate proved their net worth and solidified their place in American military history.

While many in the 1960's questioned U.S. involvement in Vietnam, including African Americans, and whether the U.S. should assume the role of world policeman, blacks nonetheless represented a substantial proportion of America's combat forces then operating in Southeast Asia (Franklin & Moss, 2000, p. 622). As America's military commitment to the region approached one-half-million men-in-arms, a subsequent draft was issued in order to augment the necessary manpower requirements, and draft cards were issued to all men black and white between the ages of 18 and 25. And while the overall percentage of blacks then residing in the U.S. was only around eleven percent, to many, it seemed a disproportionate number of young black men were to be found in America's Armed Forces. It was later revealed that approximately 30 percent of blacks who qualified were drafted contrasted with approximately only 18 percent of whites. What's more, blacks were found to be far more prone to patterns of unemployment, and were therefore often compelled to seek military service as a means by which to economically sustain themselves. At one point, black forces comprised 17 percent of all U.S. combat troops then operating in Southeast Asia, and at another point suffered a casualty rate which was commensurate to about 22 percent of the total of all U.S. casualties in that conflict (Franklin & Moss, 2000, p. 625).

While the African American community provided more than its required share to America's military commitment in Vietnam, many came to question the nation's role in the affair on both moral and philosophical grounds. Martin Luther King opposed the war on religious principles, citing "Thou shall not kill." King believed precious resources supposed to be dedicated to the principles of President Johnson's "Great Society," were being squandered instead on the battlefields of Vietnam (Franklin & Moss, 2000, p. 623). For many in the black community, the war itself held racial overtones, as it appeared to many, as further white aggression directed towards colored people half a globe away. Nevertheless, at a critical time in our nation's history, the African American elements of the society were found to "ante up" in the face of the subtleties of racism, as so often has been the case, yet rendering service, distinction and commitment to a cause many did not even believe in.

Throughout the course of America's long and colorful history of armed conflict and military engagement, blacks were to be found standing shoulder-to-shoulder with their white brothers in arms. From Bunker Hill to operation Desert Storm, African Americans have rendered invaluable service and commitment, sometimes in the face of overt discrimination, while at the same time, using the various branches of the nation's Armed Services as a platform by which to advance and elevate their cause for social and political justice. And while racism or discrimination in America's Armed Forces may not have yet been entirely abolished, wholesale integration of those forces has been achieved in a most remarkable fashion, and the African American community can reflect upon its role and contribution to that legacy with great pride. In fact, while African Americans today comprise only 12% of the total national population, they are disproportionately represented as 20% of America's armed forces (Edgerton, 2009, p. 4). To the vast majority of my students, black or white, this particular realm of the American experience serves perhaps as the least contentious; perhaps even as a possible focal point for unity, with each pointing, with great pride, towards the contributions and sacrifices made by members of their own respective race and ancestry.

CHAPTER VII

African American Family Structure and Culture

TO ME ONE of the most embarrassing aspects of teaching African American history to an overwhelming black student body was addressing the familial structure of that particular community. A structure that for much of the twentieth century was either nonexistent or sorely lacking, particularly when contrasted to white middle class America during the same period. For much of that timeframe, the saving grace of African American families could be found in two separate entities: the Church, and in African American women in general.

The Church historically taught African Americans the skills necessary to survive in a predominantly white and ever increasingly capitalistic American society. Many of the prerequisite skills necessary for success were not to be found in the recently freed black masses after their wholesale emancipation of 1865. The fundamentals necessary for the survival of the race were to be found in the Church. It was here, blacks would learn to read, write and run their own affairs devoid largely of white interference. However, the Church afforded blacks the greatest autonomy and latitude, and what little wealth that could be mustered often went into its propagation and proliferation. In some regions such as South Carolina, where the estimated number of African American Methodist Ministers in 1877 exceeded perhaps 1,000, churches and their influence in the black community increased exponentially. As one African American of the period put it, "preachin' and shouting sometimes lasted all day" (Norton, et al., 2001, p. 434). Furthermore, skills such as organizing, construction and matters of finance were simultaneously gleaned, and therefore throughout much of black America's short history of freedom, its existence has and continues to be centered around the church, as it has provided hope, structure and has ultimately and historically emerged as its saving grace.

Similarly, the African American female has emerged as a steadfast source of inspiration for generations of blacks. Since the Civil War to the present day, black women have often found themselves acting as head of the household. Even in the realm of the classroom, this historical phenomenon often held true as numerous female students were in fact, more often than not, found to be head of their respective households. Historically, it appears the African American male has emerged at times as intransigent, malcontent and sometimes altogether disinterested in the long-term progress or affairs of the family structure. Nowhere was this more evident than in the recent event touted as "The Million Man March," designed to be reflective of the more progressive views of the contemporary African American male. The march, which received an abundant degree of media attention and scrutiny, was blueprinted to attract in excess of one million black males, who were to demonstrate and reaffirm their new found values in commitment, and in support of more stable familial patterns and to coalesce in the nation's capital in order to emphasize this espoused and renewed commitment. The march, in fact, proved to be a relative failure as the anticipated numbers never manifested. (The National Park Service estimated that 400,000 people marched that day.) (McKenna, 2009, para. 29) The March was illustrative of more profound and deeply-rooted problems that have both historically, and in a contemporary context, continue today to plague and tug at the social fabric of the African American community. Black males have suffered through generations of discrimination, underemployment, and incarceration. It has even been further advocated that a black man's supposed physical endowment and voracious sexual appetite has propelled him to pursue that in which he excels, further disrupting and disabling existing family patterns. In this unstable environment, the cycle is repeated from generation to generation, as successive generations do not have effective and appropriate black male role models to emulate (Griffith, 1961, p. 90-91).

Irrespective of how these destructive patterns have emerged, it has been largely up to the African American female to provide the structure and rigidity necessary to foster successful patterns of family development. Historically, this has been achieved by women who remain closely tied to the Church, and often take on additional work such as cleaning, childcare, and whatever means that can be found at their disposal (Franklin & Moss, 2000, p. 315-317). In a more contemporary sense, the Church continues to remain as vital, but more often than not, black women have now been compelled to enter the workforce, to seek high school diplomas and even more advanced college degrees. Alternatively, they exist and subside on state, local and federal aid programs, which were initially introduced only as stop gap measures, but more often than not, now exist as permanent social service fixtures. Pronounced and prevalent patterns have developed whereby young African American females choose to have several children, often out of wedlock, in order to perpetuate sustained economic "incomes." These patterns are often crescive and destructive to the long-term well-being, and overall progress of the African American family, which, as we now know, tends to foster cycles of learned helplessness and of generational dependency.

At the present, and to the best of my knowledge, over the course of the previous three decades my in-laws have raised approximately fifty foster children with a fair proportion of those being African American. Almost always the root cause remains the destruction and lack of stability found in these minority families. Among the familiar root causes are drug abuse, multiple pregnancies, lack of income, social service intervention, and in some cases incarceration. While it is not the intention of social services or related agencies to place these minority children in the homes of middle class white Americans, it is precisely this social enclave that has the means and the wherewithal to foster or nurture the victims of this immense social problem. There tends to be an overwhelming sense within the white community that this has become a burden with which they have been saddled, in terms of the cost and overall responsibility, but one, nonetheless, the white community has largely been willing to bear.

It has been sometimes a written, and at other times an unwritten policy of America's social services networks, and more specifically child protective services to place minority children into the homes of similar ethnic families if and whenever possible. It seemed to me that most of my African American history students were in accord with this policy as perhaps the best measure by which to achieve and affect stability, and to ultimately facilitate a more well-adjusted and happy child. However, given the sheer numbers, this is not always possible. Within my own family of in-laws in the past they have at times sought to permanently adopt these children. One child in particular, a young girl whom for the purposes of anonymity I will refer to as Taheisha, was conveyed to the family, and whom the family and I had grown especially fond of, and at one juncture it did seem entirely possible that she was going to be adopted and incorporated into the family. Taheisha, the most adorable child, at times would stroke my beard and mustache and rather long hair in the most curious of fashions, painfully aware that my features were somehow distinctly different from her own. My own children at a later date performed a similar experiment while my wife and I were waiting in a local doctor's office. Two African American teenagers, who likewise were waiting most patiently, were approached by my young daughters whom after the most inquisitive and unencumbered study of their black features asked most innocently, "Why are your noses so much bigger than ours?" Finally, it was determined that the best prospects for Taheisha's success given all the adjustments that would be required if she were to be raised in a white environment, was to place her in a more "suitable" black environment, with a more conventional African American family. In accordance with past precedence, the progress of these children and future contact was rather limited, so as to prevent separation anxiety, or to reduce its impact. It was presupposed to be in Taheisha's best interest. Her subsequent removal from the family was a most painful experience but, nonetheless, deemed to be in her best interest. It was later revealed through a bizarre series of twists and turns and perhaps even one of fate, that Taheisha once again had become acquainted with the Social Services system, as both she and her sister, ultimately were to be later found in a County detention facility. The attempt to place Taheisha in the more familiar environment of a conventional black family structure apparently backfired, as Taheisha was allegedly sexually and perhaps otherwise abused by her adoptive father. The net result was that Taheisha and her sister have emerged as pawns in a destructive cycle and pattern, which has historically plagued and inhibited the advancement and promotion of healthy African

American familial structures. It is not that these destructive patterns are not to be found in other cultures, but rather they tend to be more pronounced and pervasive in African American families, which from a generational standpoint tends to be self-perpetuating.

Another black child named Darryl was likewise raised by my in-laws and was similarly a most adorable and curious child. As at that time my wife and I both worked (I was a teacher during the day and attended graduate school in the evening), my eldest daughter of pre-school age was at the same time looked after by my mother-in-law. My daughter and Darryl, born on approximately the same day and in the same hospital, grew up together as two young children, presumably unaware of their racial and cultural differences. One morning as I prepared to drop my daughter off, I was greeted by my teary eyed mother-in-law who informed me quietly in a rather subdued tone that Darryl's mother from whom he had been removed by social services had been found murdered, her body dumped along the road of a remote and rural community in southwestern New York State. I distinctly recall standing with my heart seemingly in my throat, watching the young boy play, unaware of the hand which fate had dealt him. For my own children, the experience of growing up with these minority children, was both rewarding and beneficial, especially when reinforced with my own progressive views, but for African American families, this cycle of violence and upheaval has severely undermined and retarded their social progress, in the most destructive of fashions.

Other realms of African American culture at times have proven perplexing to the white elements of American society. While embracing one's ethnic heritage is generally regarded as an inherent right and a healthy experience, this as a general rule has tended to backfire when applied to the African model or experience. The adoption of African dress and customs has often led to ridicule and pronounced chagrin by the predominant white culture. For example, the naming of children with more traditional African names such as Lakeisha, Latoya, etc., has not been viewed by mainstream American as embracing one's African culture, but instead is seen more as a rejection of the existing dominant white culture, which in turn often responds accordingly. It may even be quite possibly that African Americans have been since the 1960's making a distinctive and quantitative effort to emphasize their respective culture as more of a means of making a "political statement" or even "a social one" verses simply embracing their ancestral culture and heritage. This phenomenon, however, had already previously existed previously in American history when between 1880 and 1920 different immigrants arrived on the nation's shores from regions such as Italy, Poland, Hungary, etc., clad in traditional dress, bearing a more Catholic composition and often forming into their own ethnic enclaves (occasionally manifesting as ghettos). (Higham, 1963, p. 252). Subsequent generations of those immigrants began to reject their Central and Eastern European roots, opting instead to assimilate into the more dominant and mainstream elements of American culture. It's not that these patterns and traditions were abandoned wholesale, but rather they were assimilated and then incorporated into mainstream American culture.

African elements, however, in part due to issues relative to complexion, have often been viewed as inflammatory and non-assimilatory in nature. Nowhere has this been more evident than when a recent attempt was made to introduce or incorporate "Ebonics" into the white culture. Seldom has such rancor been evoked as when it was suggested that this black linguistic phenomenon be introduced into traditional educational programs of the nation's schools. And while I have seen similar rejections to the incorporation of alternate languages, such as Spanish, into our nation's institutions, the vehement objection to Ebonics has been striking and profound. To the white race, Ebonics continues to be viewed as abrasive, confrontational and tantamount to an outright attack or rejection of the more prevalent white culture.

One element, however, of African American culture that has made significant headway into mainstream American society is its musical contribution. Elements of rap, hip hop, and even the more traditional forms of Jazz and Rock and Roll, owe their historical roots to African music. Music of this more African genre dominates the airwaves, television screens, and entertainment industry in general, and in truth is now regarded as mainstream. Music as an art form has always been a fundamental component to African society, and similarly made the Trans Atlantic voyages of the 17th and 18th centuries (Norton, Katzman, Escott, Chudacoff, 1998, p. 349). African Americans retained this art form as a means of maintaining a link to their historical past, as a God given tool in which to communicate, to survive the nightmare and rigors of centuries of involuntary servitude, and to some extent as a means in which to endure their more contemporary circumstances. Slaves who often toiled long and arduous hours in fields, and who performed mind numbing physical tasks retained their sanity, and maintained rhythmic unity in their work flow through these melodious chords. Successive generations of African Americans would continue to embrace and foster this inexpensive and creative art form in churches, communities, events, employment, and family gatherings, and ultimately later within the entertainment industry itself.

One example of this vocal history almost entirely unknown to both blacks and whites in my classroom was the story of the Jubilee singers of Fisk University of Tennessee. The Jubilee singers provide a further testament to the importance and relevance of music as a fixture and extension of African American culture. Following the Civil War, the Jubilee singers coalesced and formed a singing entity that performed, in melodic harmony, old Negro spirituals and work songs from generations of a race held in bondage. They did this as a means by which to raise additional financial resources for the college and its primarily black constituency. (Franklin & Moss, 2000, p. 297). The first official appearance of this unique choral group at Oberlin, Ohio's Council of Congregational Churches and its success, led to additional engagements throughout the Northeast as predominantly white races flocked to hear their talented vocal abilities. Almost as a means by which to emphasize their roots as well as their meteoric progress, the troupe patterned its singing engagements in the North East to coincide with various stops along the historic Underground Railroad. Moreover, the group earned international renown as through invitation it traveled extensively playing for European audiences from England to Germany. They sang for presidents and royalty, exposing the troupe to societies with far less discriminatory overtones and even fewer racist practices. To the young black singers, the experience must have been revealing but simultaneously heart wrenching, as it probably made them painstakingly more cognizant to the overt and pervasive extent which Jim Crow existed within their own native Tennessee. Nonetheless, by 1882 the singers had managed to raise in excess of $150,000 (a sizeable sum) and helped facilitate the expansion of Fisk University. They even enabled that esteemed institute to solicit guest speakers and renowned lecturers from numerous and more diverse venues around the world.

This musical link remained a vibrant one even into the depression riddled 1930's, as groups of African American men employed by the railroad industry, referred to as "Gandy dancers," would utilize singing and rhythm as a means to lay ties and railroad track which required precision, speed and timing to construct (Gandy dancer, n.d.).

What's more, this musical legacy and the relevance of this African art form can still be seen today in the immensely popular Fox television series, "American Idol." An African American population which numbers slightly more than 10 percent of the overall U.S. population, provides an overwhelming disproportionate proclivity of singing talent unveiled on that stage. It has been advanced by some that African Americans themselves possess the physical attributes necessary to dominate this cultural avenue. In truth, it is deeply, profoundly and historically-rooted in the black experience, providing a natural means by which to both sustain, and to promote black culture through centuries of struggle.

CHAPTER VIII
Blacks in Prison

"PRISONS", IT HAS been espoused by a famous eighteenth century French philosopher, are often among the least regarded of a Nations social entities or structures, and yet sometimes can serve as a fundamental measure or yard stick of a society's overall propensity for compassion. In this spirit, few aspects of American society reflect our racial divide more than those of the nation's inherent prison programs or correctional institutions. This disproportionate representation of minority cultures is staggering to say the least. Insofar as African Americans are concerned, members of my own race have advocated that the black culture is perhaps more predisposed to be one of violence, and therefore our correctional entities are a reflection of that pattern. Moreover, it has been further advanced by some in the African American community itself, that prison is a badge of honor, and may be an additional inherent element to the concept of "*cool pose*" which as a theory or notion, is addressed more extensively in chapter ten of the text. Similarly, it was indicated to me by a member of law enforcement, that the baggy pants sometimes worn by black youths, and the manner in which they sometimes clasp the front or belt area, whereby they appear to be attempting to hold them up, is designed to mimic prison issued garb, which when dispensed often tends to be rather ill-fitting. To address this apparent disparity in numbers and other related issues of blacks in prison, I have solicited the assistance of my friend and long time colleague, Thomas Dryja, a former police officer, New York State corrections officer and current criminal justice professor of the college where I presently teach, in addition to the personal opinions and reflections of several close sources within the law enforcement community itself.

Mr. Dryja, a former corrections employee, worked as a jail deputy for seven years (November 1971-February 1978) for the Erie County New York Sheriff's Department; and, as a police officer for 22 years within a large suburban police department outside the city of Buffalo (1978-2000). During this time, Dryja gained important insights giving him unique perspectives relative to the incarceration of the black male.

According to Tom, law enforcement more often than not is the black male's first point of contact within the criminal justice system. New York State is relatively the same as throughout all of the U.S., as junior officers are usually placed in the worst or most crime laden of precincts or districts. They are often made to work the least desirable shifts, either afternoons or midnights, which by tradition, tend to produce the most violent and stressful calls per tour of duty. Now, these inexperienced officers, more often have not developed the people skills or street smarts yet, but nonetheless are being placed predominately in the lower income, inner city areas. Think of it, suggests Dryja, with the exception of the military, no other employer puts their least experienced workers into the most critical of job environments. Taking into account the middle-class flight, both black and white out of those cities, and the prevalence of young officers, there is a high probability of street encounters going bad. The people and communication skills needed here are often to be developed "on the fly" so to speak, so as to make bad situations worse and moreover to make the possibility of any good situations going bad as well. In other words, knowing the sometimes aggressive nature and the predisposition of these new police recruits to affect an arrest without first attempting to administer other forms of "street justice" often at their disposal, the number of arrests is therefore magnified in these minority areas, a point as it turns out which was often attested to by my students.

Furthermore, Dryja asserts, that before one can study why black males are over-represented in jail, one must look first at how they got there. It is also necessary to examine the type of patrol strategies used to fight crime and most importantly, where and whom are these strategies being directed towards. By studying police, their tactics and patterns, it is possible to formulate a rationale on this apparent disproportion. One tactic often used by law enforcement is Saturation Patrol, which is precisely what the name implies. Police sometimes increase the number of officers to remedy or control a particular problem, whether real or perceived. Saturated Patrol is used primarily for specific events like concerts, festivals, or dignitary protection or used to cover or saturate a particular area, district or precinct due to an increase in crime or disorder. In its latter use it often means deploying into the crime ridden inner cities, low income or urban areas, which are often dominated by minorities. Due to the basic elements of Saturated Patrols, their frequent car stops, its numerous street encounters and its zero tolerance practices, and by its very nature of being in inner cities, it nearly guarantees that the number of black males arrested will be at a much higher rate than white males. Moreover the low chance of a black male making bail due to their income status, and their public and political environment, will in all probability add to his overall time spent waiting in jail, or awaiting trial.

Another police tactic sometimes employed is Target Patrols. Unlike Saturated Patrols, Target Patrols target particular crimes or individual gang members. Used again primarily in low income urban areas, these patrols usually target quality of life crimes, such as open container, public intoxication, and loud music violations, and crimes associated with low income minorities who often do not have the money, transportation or resources to get out of the area. Target Patrols also single out drug and weapons violators, again, often found on the street level in your lower income urban areas. A common denominator within Saturated or Target Patrols is that both tactics are acceptable and safe from a public relations standpoint, as their intended targets are often minority or the economically disadvantaged, and therefore they don't infringe upon your more affluent neighborhoods or towns which more often than not tend to be white in orientation.

An additional element or tactic is your Street Crime or Tactical Patrol Units. Focusing again on high crime or problem neighborhoods, the officers who usually comprise these units are generally handpicked for their arrest and street encounter aggressiveness. Acting often like legally sanctioned vigilantes, it is their primary job to arrest, detain and otherwise "legally harass" those perceived undesirables. By legally harassing, it effects stops, questions, or otherwise warns those whom the police officer perceives as potential suspects or jail clients, to let them know that "we are here," and "we know who you are." Used rarely in your higher end urban or suburban neighborhoods, these highly motivated Police Officers often serve as a uniformed "Neighborhood Watch Groups" with legal credentials. The City of Buffalo in the 1970's had a Tactical Patrol Unit of hand-picked police officers who were known for their numerous arrests and physical bearing. They wore lightning bolts on their leather jackets, which were also found to be painted on their patrol cars.

In the 1950's, Buffalo had a special unit referred to as the Flying Squad. Unofficially, however, it was called the "Turban Squad" because most of its arresting officers appeared in court with their heads wrapped and bandaged due to injuries sustained during arrests. Other police tactics used in concert with "get tough" legislation and the war on crime, resulted in a 70% increase in the percentile of arrests and incarcerations, and can be broken down as follows; violent offenders increased 55%, drug offenders 21%, and projects and public order offenders 24%. By the end of 2008, 2.1 million adult Americans will be behind bars, with many of those being minorities or African Americans.[**]

Another such tool obtained from legislation are the School Zone Drug Laws, enforced in various states and often resulting in harsher penal sanctions for those violators. Most suburban school systems are consolidated. The Caucasian student body is bused into its more centralized location, resulting in fewer individual school locations and less police coverage. Inner city school structures conversely, tend to be minority-dominated and less centralized, usually being disbursed across an area of the city. This warrants then more police coverage under existing school drug laws. In turn, we find higher arrest rates in those minority environments, which means, as a general rule, that they (minorities) are more adversely affected by current legislation.

An additional instrument at the disposal of law enforcement is the development of Community Narcotic Enforcement Teams. There are five regional teams that combat street level drug trafficking and related crimes. In 2007, there were 1790 undercover drug purchases resulting in 1451 drug arrests, again mostly in poor urban centers. Also, the New York State Police Gun Investigation Unit targets illegal street use and sale primarily of weapons involving specific crimes resulting in 641 arrests, again from within those pervasively minority areas (in 2007). Therefore, what we can conclude, and what this tells us, Dryja suggests, is the police and their tactics are often made to

---

[**]   Source Bureau of justice statistic's prisoners in 2007.

order or designed towards singling out black males, not because of racism, but rather as procedures, whose net effect tends to assure that the black population will more often than not, become the majority in the nation's jails, holding centers and prisons. The inability to escape their environment, in concert with police and bail practices, and the added inability to afford dream team attorneys, is a made to order recipe for arrest and an increase in the overall black jail population. According to Dryja, statistics indicate that the instances of incarceration increase exponentially, if you are unable to make bail. It is estimated one in eight black males between the ages of 25-27 are in prison. Moreover, black males are imprisoned at a rate of 6%, which is seven times greater than that of white males (3405 blacks to 465 whites per 100,000 inmates respectfully.)[***] Furthermore, black males account for 38% of all violent offenses yet, are only less than 12% of the total population. In New York State, the total prison population is 62,599 with drug offenses accounting for nearly fourteen thousand of those incarcerated.[****]

Moreover, Mr. Dryja continued, it is necessary to explore the concept of jail and correctional institutions themselves. Most people as a rule, he suggests, don't want to go to jail, but rather look upon it as an occupational risk, or as the byproduct of a moment of weakness, stress, emotion or otherwise. Much as in civilized society, it is sometimes how and when you adapt, that can make all the difference between success and failure, or in terms of jail; even one of life or death, whether real, perceived or even from a psychological standpoint.

During the process of incarceration, Dryja reminds us, the fortunate ones adapt almost immediately, but for the vast majority it becomes a learning, and sometimes painful, experience. The less fortunate become chum bait for the ever lurking population of jail sharks. Dryja began his seven year jail career right after the infamous Attica riot and concluded it in February of 1978 when, in his estimation, jails became holding centers and when prisoners began to petition with regularity for their alleged or supposed prisoner rights. An approximate breakdown of the inmates in the

---

[***] Source: Paige Harrison and Allen Beck, Prisoners in 2003, Washington D.C., Bureau of Justice Statistics, 2004, pg 9.

[****] Source: NYS Department of Criminal Justice Service, these statistics allow us to look at jails and prisons and the black male experience.

Erie County Holding Center at that time were estimated as follows; by cell block:

A & AA	100 % black male
B	60 % black male–16-18 years old
BB	100 % black male–16-18 years old
C	35 % black male
CC	50 % black male
I	35 % black male–16-18 years old
II	10 % black male–16-18 years old
J	40 % black male * {Note: This was used for federal prisoners as well}
JJ	40 % black male

Roughly 57% of those incarcerated were black males, and if one includes the female population, the overall percentage now approaches nearly 60%. The city of Buffalo, Dryja continued, at this time had an African American population of only about 25%. After the infamous Attica riot (September 1971), corrections systems as we knew them would never again be the same. A new breed of inmate with their own ideology was emerging, young, black, political and increasingly radical, and professing to be "political prisoners," rather than products of a criminal justice system. Islam was taking root among black male militant inmates then, culminating in Malcolm X's murder, and as Dryja tells his correctional students, "Attica wasn't about escape, it was about prisoner's rights, the changing of the guard so to speak from the old lock step policies of the 1930's-1960's, to a younger, smarter, and city wise inmate who no longer accepted the practices of the past and was now seeking political and social redress." The right to practice any religion, discipline hearings, law libraries, medical care, special housing, and care for the emotionally disturbed or sociopath were now petitioned for with regularity and sometimes even demanded. The inmate culture, according to Tom, in an inverted way, often mirrors our own in many respects, in that the black male, once a minority on the outside, is now, within the prison structure, the majority, and thus responds accordingly. "Blacks, once on the lower rungs of the social ladder, now emerge as the police, the politicians, and the ones who sometimes administer justice, and whom at times you must now go to for protection." The black male thus, has successfully accomplished, by manipulating his prison environment, that which he was unable to accomplish on the outside over the course of the past several centuries. What's more, he now emerges as the elite, the power broker, the "man." Again, states Dryja, "let's not lose sight of the fact that nobody wants to go to jail, but the black male, taking into account the aforementioned, and the fact that he has successfully been integrated into a society where he's no longer the beggar, does provide him a more advantageous set of circumstances by which to both manipulate and to control to some extent his own environment."

Working the cell block for seven years, Dryja also observed a few differences in the ability of the black male to adapt over that of his white counterparts. The extensive use of the word "brother," to someone who was not an actual blood relation, did nonetheless tend to form a strong bond, or, if not that, at least one of recognition between the black males. The term "brother" was seldom used by whites held in incarceration. There is a certain pronounced caste system that was readily incorporated into the black male population. It often corresponded with the arrest charges or prior convictions one had. The status one held and the respect one commanded was generally commensurate with your place in that hierarchy. Another difference was that your black inmate, according to Tom, had basically the same complaints or problems that white prisoners had, but the black male usually attempted to work them out with each other for the common good. Inadequate legal counsel, health problems, visitation problems, it appeared to Dryja as if they had coalesced or formed their individual blocks into communal ones, or even as unofficial labor units, whereas the white males seldom merged with one voice, rarely worked together, and for the most part tended to be loners.

Furthermore, Dryja suggested, it is equally important to examine an otherwise forgotten group, the teenage criminal, with a particular emphasis on the black male teen. First and foremost, for Dryja, 1971 was a significant time for several interesting reasons; first, the Attica fiasco occurred right in "his own back yard." Secondly, in 1971-72, the City of Buffalo simultaneously recorded the highest rate of homicides in its entire history. Generally speaking, most all black male teenaged gang members were in one or more of the following gang's: the Pythons, the Mad Dogs, the Aliah Turks, or the Manhattan Lovers. And third, when Dryja began working as a Jail Deputy in the Erie County Holding Center, the gang's of the 1970's in Western New York area were often far different from those of today. The gang's then were formed for turf solidarity, and for the need to belong to something. Drugs, prostitution, property offenses weren't then at their core, but a willingness to kill someone not in your gang, neighborhood or even random and wanton killings for no reason other than being different was a common component or thread. Also during this period, a dramatic upswing in the number of homicides committed by white teen males was observed. These white teen killers unlike their black teen counterparts were sometimes extremely violent in their acts usually conducted in concert with a heinous crime such as kidnapping, robbery, burglary, or assault. These killings often weren't gang related, but rather singular hits. What these killers did, however, have in common was they usually came from a broken home. Similarly, they were poor and usually they came from an inner city or urban area. More often than not, they had dropped out of school, or were only attending in order to recruit additional gang members. Similarly, most had no parental guidance, and were usually street wise by the age of eight or nine. Finally, states Dryja, nearly all had previous or prior contact with the criminal justice system, with little or no subsequent follow-up by those authorities. Dryja's constant dealings with the black teenage inmate's led him to conclude that jails were not to be found as punishment, or as a scarlet letter, but rather as a refuge from the street. Prison, Dryja believes, had become "a place to renew old acquaintances and a relatively safe haven or environment when contrasted to the street."

Another striking difference between the adult black males incarcerated versus the black teen, was that teens without exception, appeared to Dryja to have no concept of punishment or as to what a life sentence meant. They either didn't attach a meaning to being gone for 25 years or more, or perhaps says Dryja, they were unable to grasp the concept of time, and that they would in all probability be in their late 40's before they would ever possibly see freedom again. Perhaps due to their environment, or even their life style, they couldn't relate it seems to a Florida vacation, a home in the suburbs, little league baseball, or even eating at a fine restaurant. Their world often was a violent one, where the life expectancy might only be 21 or 22 years old, and one in which street respect was your reward for life. You can't miss that which you do not have, or do not know. A case in point, while working {BB} Block, one of Dryja's 17-year-old inmates returned from a sentencing for two homicides, and received a sentence of 25 years to life. On his part, according to Tom, "no remorse, no concern, or no worry, was to be found, but rather telling anyone who would listen, that when he gets out he (black inmate) is going to kill those witnesses who testified against him."

An additional aspect pointed out by Dryja, was that unlike the adult black male inmate, the black male teen generally didn't abuse alcohol or drugs, which was quite the opposite from the white male teen, who often used drugs and alcohol with regularity. Black teen males were relatively substance abuse free; "it just wasn't part of their street culture." Like the adult black male, black teens sought to create informational social and support networks in jail. Just like white male adults, however, white teens tended also to be loners. Within these "family" groupings, the black prison community provided support, protection, counseling and mentors for each other. An additional characteristic was that the suicide rate, during Tom's seven year time at the jail was significantly higher for white males than it was for black males, which quite possibly was attributed to those support mechanisms of the black males in jail, to their easier transition, adjustment to jail, or even possibly just knowing their future and probable outcome. Statistics show that first time offenders, middle class, upper class or otherwise, that white males largely appeared as weak or feminine, and that those labeled as sexual abusers, are often at far greater risk for suicide, all attribute's most black male inmates generally do not possess. But what those statistics, however, cannot explain, states Dryja, is that at one time or another black inmates may have previously exhibited some of those same traits, but often by their second incarceration, or through their ability to network, are usually more successful in their ability to integrate and favorably adapt, and usually therefore, tend to have lower suicide rates than their white counterparts. Uniform Crime Reports and other statistics, as well as victim surveys can give us these numbers, suggests Dryja, but once stated often incorporate "small lies, big lies, and those statistics and how their crimes are reported, can be both officer or victim biased, or even politically skewed" as they are often relative to the reporting Police Department, departmental goals or even the community itself.

What I was able to glean from my colleague was that most if not all social studies pertaining to the nature of crime and its principles are subjective, and therefore, it was Dryja's hope that through his own career experiences in corrections and in law enforcement, to provide the reader "a unique perspective and insight into the nation's criminal justice systems and the mechanisms by which they operate." What conclusions we can gather is that law enforcement, specifically its tactics and goals, often has a direct relationship or bearing on just who gets arrested. Moreover, the subject's social and economic background can largely affect not only the quality of legal safeguards he gets, but also his perceived entitlement from the criminal justice community is similarly and largely based upon one's social status. "We shouldn't overlook the adaptability of the black male," states Dryja, "it isn't that he has some hidden criminal chromosome or simply because of his race that he is more likely to become a criminal, but, rather his ready and built-in ability to bond, and to enter the prison life style as an equal, where he now becomes the ruling entity, the leader, and the decision maker." Finally, language, culture, and other common threads found inherent in criminal structures, have been documented thousands of times; broken homes, drugs, gangs, and no direction, remain the common denominators, but additionally and perhaps equally important is, if the concept of punishment has no meaning for you, or similarly, if you have no goals, no new experiences, or even quality of life, jail then, is just a stopping point in a more protracted journey that in the end, usually leads to nowhere. Thus incarcerating sanctions, and their overall meaning and impact are dramatically altered or substantially mitigated. As Tom recounted, he liked to compare it to a Seinfeld episode, whereby Jerry and Elaine purchase two plane tickets, but the only two tickets they had left weren't together, one was in coach and the other in first class. In deciding who gets what ticket, Jerry asked Elaine if she ever sat in first class before, she replies, "no." Jerry then remarks, "then you won't know what you are missing," so Jerry took the first class ticket leaving Elaine sitting in coach. Over saturation of law enforcement, urban police tactics, legislative sanctions aimed at the African American community, so often one of no goals, no experience, no jobs, a 2009 recession, and negative job growth, all are tantamount to a formula that will likely result in the further imprisonment of the black male.

To much of my collective African American student body, it seemed to me they were either embarrassed or ashamed by this cultural phenomenon, but some I believe were angry. It wasn't that the numbers were in dispute, but rather those numbers appear as skewed possibly due to practices of law enforcement whose programs, may not be intrinsically racial, but nonetheless, whose net or cumulative effect ultimately leads to racial inequity in our nation's criminal justice systems. One law enforcement official in the Buffalo area conveyed to me an incident whereby he attended a police sensitivity training seminar that was mandated by his department. It was at this seminar, the instructor asked each officer to explain why they had chosen law enforcement as a career. One African American Lieutenant stepped forward and responded that he "did so in order that he might no longer be harassed by white officers in his own community." Moreover, one inmate I recently interviewed incarcerated formerly in the Attica State Correctional Facility, indicated to me that as a young white male then in his late twenties, he did not on the inside, feel the racial pressures that he encountered while living on the outside in an inner city neighborhood within the city of Buffalo itself. The prevailing sense among both of the races then incarcerated, was that irrespective of their cultural differences, both were simultaneously being subjected to the wrath of the "man." Finally, in all fairness, a current Buffalo policeman and former member of the "Flying or Turban" squad or Tactical Patrol unit indicated to me that if any suspects or police personnel appeared in court wearing bandages, it was only because those perpetrators vehemently resisted arrest or being taken into custody.

Therefore, it would seem that societal patterns relative to the disparaging numbers of blacks in prison more readily lend themselves or at least tend to be more reflective of social and environmental concerns, than to that of any potential or presupposed genetic predisposition. What's more and what is clear, is that these numbers while disparaging represent one more great racial and cultural divide, which continues to both erode and to undermine the nation's social infrastructure.

CHAPTER IX
Geography and Race

WHILE TEACHING AMERICAN history and government in Central and Eastern Europe following the collapse of the former Soviet Union, I was sometimes astounded and simultaneously embarrassed when issues pertaining to race were raised by my students (who as it turned out often had enormous insights into American historical trends). Promoting the American system as a model for these newly emerging democracies to emulate, it was sometimes painful to convey that on the cusp of a new millennium, America was yet geographically separated,–and this, more than 140 years after the issuance of the Emancipation Proclamation. Blacks have largely emerged as the inhabitants of the nation's inner cities, while whites dominate the more expansive affluent peripheral suburbs and surrounding rural communities. This state of geographic and economic segregation was not designed, but nonetheless exists as a striking manifestation of our nation's social and moral points of view. The processes which have led us to this apparent state of segregation was also addressed in my African American class as part of my plan to present a fair and balanced representation on all matters of race. A long-time friend of the family and prominent member of the National Rifle Association has even gone so far as to indicate to me, that it is his belief that America's cities have emerged as nothing short of "prisons" designed to keep the black race penned up in those respective areas.

At the turn of the century, The Urban League, a spin-off of the N.A.A.C.P., was created to aid and assist African Americans, who early in the twentieth century were moving in vast numbers to the urban and cosmopolitan centers of the North in the midst of the forces of industrialization that were then sweeping the region (Franklin & Moss, 2000, p. 342). Jobs were abound, and as such represented real and potential opportunity to the black masses seeking to escape the oppressive political and economic circumstances of the more stagnant South. For most African Americans this also represented not only demographic, but more visceral cultural changes, from a rural, to a more urban lifestyle. If there was already a preexisting condition of racial divide among the races, a new geographical element was being sewn into the American social fabric. In successive generations the overall landscape of America's great cities would soon thereafter be permanently altered, as African Americans would begin to populate those centers in great preponderance. Within the time span of two world wars (largely in order to meet American wartime production demands) the complexion of America's great cities and industrial centers became more reflective of that social shift. Within two successive decades following World War II, there would be an exodus of the once dominant white culture to suburban and rural areas, leaving a vacuum that would be filled by a progressive and expanding black population. In many instances, the previously dominant white community with its wealth would largely abandon these former bustling centers of commerce. In other instances, whites held onto their inner city dwellings, instead choosing to rent to the more credit and asset starved black masses. Due in part, perhaps to human nature, an old adage exists suggesting that people will not care for that which they do not own. In short, those African Americans renting often had no stake or vested interest since the homes and businesses did not belong to them. Within a few short years America's cities became synonymous with poverty and depredation (becoming a manifestation of that adage), and the segregation of the races was once again achieved. The continued abandonment of our nation's cities and infrastructures, and their subsequent deterioration provided an immense impetus and an abundant source of wide ranging opinions among my students.

The prevailing sense of the black students was that our cities have indeed been abandoned, and that due in part to the extrication of white wealth and resources, governmental intervention and programs became necessary in order to restore the economic vitality, or to some extent parity with the more affluent white suburban areas. Moreover, there tends to be a degree of latent hostility on the part of blacks who believed that whites only recently relinquished their control of these inner city dwellings and properties when they were already in an advanced state of neglect or disrepair. The prevailing opinion of white students is that the rapid deterioration of those respective areas has been achieved by years of abuse and an overall lack of initiative, commitment and pride. These two interpretations of the issue at hand could not stand in more stark opposition to one another. What is certain is that a new dimension and component has been introduced into the overall problem of America's race relations, and deep divisions now exist between the urban and suburban sectors of our nation. Within a few short years America's cities became synonymous with poverty and depredation. The segregation of the races was again being affected.

To underscore this point, I have conveyed to successive classes some of the programs which have been implemented in and around the numerous suburban communities surrounding the Buffalo metropolitan area, which many believe have been designed to discourage black or urban migration to these more affluent areas. To be fair, building codes in these ascribed municipalities tend to be cumbersome and restrictive in nature. What is particularly vexing is the extent to which many have attached square footage addendums as prerequisites to the issuance of new building permits. On the surface, these requirements appear rather innocuous, but in reality darker and more duplicitous motives are to be found inextricably linked to these requirements. According to the US Census Bureau a typical home in the 1970s-1980s ranged between 1,500 to 1,800 square feet (U.S. Census Bureau, 2010, chart).

However, as of late, many of the building codes require newly-constructed homes to be in excess of 2,000 square feet. Statistics bear this out, by 2005, the median house was 2,227 square feet (U.S. Census Bureau, 2010, chart). To give the reader a point of reference, my own suburban home (a 2-story colonial) is just slightly under 2,000 square feet consisting of five bedrooms, kitchen, one bath, dining room, and a nearly 30 foot in length living room, to say nothing of a fully remodeled basement which does not even figure in to the square footage factor. A home in excess of more than 2,000 square feet tends to be rather large in breadth, and, in most instances, cost prohibitive. And that is precisely the point as families of limited means, or on the lower end of the socio-economic spectrum can ill afford these homes, and often those families are to be found in the African American community. Regardless of the intent, whether by design or more innocuous reasons, the net effect is to generally exclude or at least limit minority immigration into the more affluent suburban communities.

In a related matter, an event occurred which I have only recently shared with some of my students. A family member of mine purchased a house in an affluent, predominately white, suburban neighborhood in the metropolitan Buffalo area. My wife, children and I were extended an invitation to visit the new residence, and were given a personal tour after which we all gathered in the new kitchen for refreshments. At this juncture a conversation ensued and my wife pointed out that one of her closest friends and colleagues, a middle aged African American woman, had only recently purchased a house in the same neighborhood. The friend was now experiencing immense difficulty in finding acceptance in the community. One evening, the friend returned home to find a rock thrown through her rear sliding glass door, and while there was no note attached she nonetheless gleaned a message from this most malicious act.

Shortly thereafter, on a Sunday afternoon, after attending church services the woman in question and her sister stopped at a nearby convenient store in order to purchase a cup of coffee. Prior to entering the establishment the two women were momentarily engaged in a conversation still seated in the car, when police arrived on the scene ordering the two women from the vehicle. According to the authorities, a 9-1-1 call was received presupposing the two women as possibly "casing out" the establishment for what may have been a potential robbery. This precipitous act was the final straw in compelling this poor woman and her family, who only recently abandoned the city of Buffalo for what they hoped might be a better quality of life, to once again return to the inner city and its more familiar social patterns.

As for the family member who had just purchased his home, the recounting of these events elicited little if any sympathy towards this black woman and her family. My wife, who anticipated at least some measure of compassion to be displayed towards her displaced friend, was appalled at the subsequent response. As we sat collectively around the kitchen table of, the following was offered, "I'm not surprised. She doesn't belong here." Almost immediately I vociferously objected. I stated explicitly that every citizen of this great country has every legal and moral right to reside wherever they so choose. The most torrid of discussions followed. My wife joined in the chorus and quipped that she was appalled by such an overtly racial comment and that she expected an apology. None was forthcoming. Moreover, a member of my family continued by suggesting that "He had worked his entire life in order to get out of the city and to get away from those people." He believed they were now following him into the suburbs, diminishing not only his quality of life, but that of his property value as well. His objection was adamant. He added that I myself had no right to judge him as I did not grow up with "those people." As such, I was not subjected to the intimidation and ostracism white people who were forced to live in black neighborhoods of the inner city were forced to suffer. At this point, my wife and I decided it was prudent to gather the children and to depart from the residence post haste.

I was certain that I was right in my moral convictions, but on that long and introspective ride home, I remained disturbed about his last comment. Did I as a young man who grew up in suburban and quasi-rural white America, have the right to pass judgment upon the mores and social instincts of someone who grew up in that more contentious environment? I tried to place myself in those shoes and, most admittedly they were not comfortable. Given all the turmoil that had occurred in his life, the fights and overwhelming humiliation, I would in all probability be unable to assuage his anger or resentment. I was neither raised in that environment, nor was I subject to similar patterns in thought. Therefore, due in part to the education and learning of my formative years, I came to embrace more progressive and enlightened views on matters of race. As for the family member in question, he continues to harbor racial biases, having even been sent home from his employer due to physical altercations with African Americans.

Another illustration of this prevalent geographical divide for me had intense personal ramifications. As a 23-year veteran and officer of a suburban fire department only once in all of those years did we receive an application from an African American candidate. As was customary an individual's application was brought before the collective governing body in which the proposed application was then read before the company as a whole. The typical course of action was for a background investigation to be conducted by officers of that body, after which a discussion ensued, to then be followed by a collective company vote.

On one Thursday evening in particular the proposed application of an African American was laid on the table before the company.

Almost immediately, both the side and rear doors were closed and in rather hushed tones it was revealed that the applicant in question was African American, and a general opinion from the company was solicited. Much to my chagrin the company objected almost in unison to the proposed membership of the applicant, with the president of the body even joking about the fried chicken fund raising barbeques the company might hold in the future. Due in part to my convictions, and in part that I would not be able to face my students, I objected most vociferously. Moreover, I exhorted my displeasure, even berating the company for this most overt racial bias and equally appalling behavior. There was a moment of extreme and immense discomfort which followed, the likes of which I would care not to experience again. Suddenly a colleague of mine, a man of the most intimidating physique, rose from his chair and similarly began to reprimand the company. After further company debate our intercession proved for naught, as the company simply voted to override our objections and the applicant was rejected. It was later learned that the individual in question had been previously arrested, which was then used as the pretext by which to dismiss the application altogether.

Attitudes of animosity were displayed towards my colleague and me for sometime thereafter. One of my duties at the fire station was to wear an air pack for interior fire attack, and after returning from a fire call one evening, the colleague whom had bravely stood by my side, expressed some concern that given the prevailing and latent animosity, he feared we might not be "backed" up in a critical situation. I summarily dismissed this thought, but that it should even be entertained is extraordinarily telling. Even to the present with a departmental roster exceeding 100 active firefighters, not one to my knowledge is African American.

Irrespective of root causes during the fluid and progressive migration patterns of the 20th century, America has reemerged as an increasingly segregated society, with blacks in overwhelming preponderance inhabiting our nation's inner cities, and with the vast majority of the white population clamoring to coalesce in the more affluent suburban and rural areas. This can neither be remediated through the forced integration of our schools or affirmative action programs. The fact that I, a white suburban college professor, was solicited to teach black history to a largely black constituency in an inner city college is further reflective or indicative of this pattern.

In a related matter, my wife and I were recently on a business trip to the downtown area of Pittsburgh, and while there we decided to visit that city's Heinz Center of History. The distance to that facility was nearly two miles from our hotel, so we solicited a shuttle bus to the museums destination. The driver (himself an African American) inquired as to where we were from, whereby we responded almost in unison that we were in fact from "Buffalo, NY". To our astonishment, he abruptly retorted, "No you're not", and proceeded to indicate that we were from the surrounding suburbs, and what's more, he even correctly identified the precise neighboring town in which we reside. The point was not that our driver was in possession of any gifted psychic or telepathic capabilities, but rather having previously lived in the area he was painfully aware of the existing geographical divide inherent to that region and a fixture so often found endemic to many of America's great and sprawling urban centers.

CHAPTER X

Prejudice, Presupposition and Profiling

DISCRIMINATION IT SEEMS to me can be taught, learned, experienced or may even be an intrinsic component and exist as a fundamental element of our overall character. A publication known as <u>Warrens Common School Geography</u> used by primary school children at the conclusion of the Civil War incorporated just such a component in its 1866 edition:

> "It is fortunate for our country that the Spaniards (who discovered the New World) first landed at the South, leaving the Atlantic coast of North America to be chiefly settled by the English. The Spaniards were cruel and avaricious . . . the people of the Spanish colonies, therefore, became idle, ignorant and corrupt; and their decedents retain that character to this day. But the English were an industrious people, who loved liberty and humanity, and earned success by energetic toil in the fields and on the sea."

Entire generations of American school children were taught these discriminatory presuppositions.

Even as a school teacher and later as a college professor, in my over twenty years of teaching, I myself would sometimes struggle to overcome this somewhat inherent fixture. I recall while teaching on the seventh and eighth grade levels, a teacher from the lower grade would occasionally warn me about certain students who would now be entering my particular grade. This insider information would sometimes leave me with presupposed elements of discrimination towards a student I had not yet even met. More often than not, I have found this "insider" information to be erroneous and often counter-productive. Even on the college level, colleagues of mine in faculty room discussions will attempt to give me a proverbial heads up, apprising me of students who they believe to be possibly cheating on exams, or who have supposed negative behavioral patterns. In some of my classes, especially in my African American class, in the face of sometimes overt and outward manifestations of hostility, I often made a conscious effort not to ascertain the name on a student paper (research, mid-term, final exam or otherwise) which were generally essay in structure and subjective in nature. In this manner, by not being cognizant of the student's name, I could be more balanced and objective and thus eliminate this built-in aspect towards discrimination when grading those papers. If these predetermining factors are to be found in something as fundamental as our nation's educational system, it is hardly surprising that these elements might remain as prevalent in the everyday discourses of our society as a whole.

In the winter of 2000, my family and I had decided to take a trip from Buffalo to Nashville, Tennessee in order to visit an Aunt and Uncle during the winter recess break. I had recently endured two surgeries (one a hernia and the other a torn rotator cuff) resulting in my arm being placed in a sling and my walking with a substantial limp. Having only had these surgeries less than a week before our trip, my wife was chosen to drive. We headed south making our way through Pennsylvania, Ohio, and into Kentucky, and after approximately eight hours of driving, we approached the city of Louisville. Not making especially good time, and with hours of driving yet ahead of us, we decided to stop only briefly at a local McDonalds, so as to be able to get back on the road again quickly. The weather being rather inclement, we quickly slipped on our jackets and coats, mine being a Confederate wool cavalry jacket with the ranking stripes of a Sergeant and accentuated with brass buttons (the type frequently worn by Civil War re-enactors). My students are accustomed to seeing me in this garb as I have a blue Union Lieutenant's Infantry jacket as well, and wear both of them frequently, primarily out of my love for history and particularly all things related to the Civil War. As I entered the McDonald's (with limp and arm in sling) I must have looked like a survivor from General Pickett's ill-fated 1863 frontal assault at Gettysburg. My wife proceeded to the counter with our daughters to place the order, and I opted instead to sit at a table and wait for their return. Suddenly, a group of African American males, for a reason that at that moment I could not ascertain, began focusing their attention in my direction. As they stood and approached my table, I suddenly became aware of my jacket and realized that it must have been altogether offensive to them. They began to circle and coalesce around me and while they spoke not a word, it was apparent their intentions were less than friendly. For what seemed an eternity, we glanced at one another in the most hostile fashion, but what perhaps concerned me the most aside from being out numbered, was that in my present physical condition I could in no way adequately defend myself. As my wife and daughters returned with the purchase in hand, they too became aware that something was awry. I told my wife to take the girls and to leave immediately, she hesitated at first but I reiterated as if it were almost a command to return to the car and get help if possible. As my wife was beginning to make her way to the car, a white couple who I had never met before, perforated the circle, approached the table and began to converse with me as though I was an old long lost friend. "Tom" they said, "how have you been, it's been a long time." As we continued to converse over the next five or ten minutes, the circle of seemingly hostile black males began to loosen and then melt away. These intervening angels who watched the whole incident unfold, must have been equally aware of the offensive nature of my jacket. Long hair, Confederate jacket, was this "cracker" trying to make a political statement? It simply was a manifestation of my affection for all things historical, but to these men of color, it invoked inherent prevalent and discriminatory aspects and probably was indeed offensive. Strangely enough, only eighteen hours later I was to be found in the home of a beautiful middle-aged African American woman, "best friend and neighbor," to my Aunt and Uncle, discussing over a cold drink, her extensive native African art collection, the Harlem Renaissance and the famed Sojourner Truth. Silently I kept mulling over to myself, "only in America, only in America."

Several years ago I made a trip to central Ohio with two close friends of mine, whom I regard as being very progressive and well informed on matters of race. My friends and I over the years have held numerous discussions relating to matters of race and social injustice, and I believed that I had a relative understanding on their views. The trip was designed so that we might meet with two individuals who were towing a motorcycle from somewhere west of Ohio, in order that they could trade the motorcycle for a classic car that was brought by my friends and me. We arrived at the pre-determined designation first, and awaited their arrival, while waiting we decided to order lunch and were approximately half way through the meal, when a phone call interrupted us. My friend selling the vehicle had a brief discussion with the individuals whom we were to meet. "They'll be here in five minutes," he said as we completed our meal. "They're a couple of black guys," he continued. Immediately I questioned him on this. "How can you tell?" I asked. "You can just tell," he responded. "You can just tell?" I reiterated. "Yeah, absolutely." At which point my second friend interjected, "You can most definitely tell." It was explained to me that their speech patterns and mannerisms often betray who an individual is. "And this can be gleaned even over the telephone?" I asked. I shook my head disapprovingly and continued to finish my meal when the trailer, motorcycle, and alleged "black guys" arrived. My friends left me, departing to talk business with the men in question.

Completing a second cup of coffee, I proceeded to join my friends in the parking lot and much to my delight, I found the two gentlemen not to be African American, but rather both were middle-aged Caucasian men. I couldn't afford to miss this opportunity and proceeded to stroll up to my friends, and said in not so subtle tones, "So I see you met your two black guys." All the way home, I continued to humorously lambaste them, but both held firm that as a general rule you can indeed ascertain someone's ethnic roots simply through patterns of speech. While this may be a form of presupposed discrimination, it is often not affected through malicious practices, but more often through learned and acquired experiences.

Similarly, from many of my own African American students who display the utmost chagrin regarding my presence in the classroom, so too had previous experiences caused them to presuppose that a white male teacher, would presumably be largely disaffected and disenfranchised from their historical experiences and cultural norms. One black woman approximately thirty years in age could never quite seem to get past this presupposed element as she never missed an opportunity in which to display to me her immense displeasure at my being ascribed the role of her mentor and educator. Upon seeing my motorcycle helmet on the desk, she inquired as to whether that was my motorcycle parked in front of and adjacent to the college. Already knowing the answer, she proceeded to inform me that I could not park there and she would tell security of the matter in order to affect its removal. Night after night she would glare at me with the most hostile countenance, and no measure of knowledge relating to the African American experience displayed by me seemed to assuage her anger. I struggled most ardently to continue to win her over, painfully aware that the sum total of all her past experiences and racial predispositions might yet prevail over intelligence, logic and reason.

An October article of a college publication entitled <u>The Chronicle of Higher Education (2008)</u> indicated that "A disproportionate number of black males never graduate from high schools and we can no longer simply say this is not our problem." From my own observation, this assertion is disturbingly correct. In my own college classroom, the ratio of black females to black males was approximately two to one. Moreover, it seemed to me African American females sometimes exhibited a subtle and subliminal degree of hostility toward their male counterparts. Generally speaking, African American women did outperform their male colleagues and yet one black male student of mine (a foreign exchange student from continental Africa) did not fit the mold. He exhibited few, if any, similar cultural and educational traits of the other black males. It bothered me that I could not account for this anomaly, but an article in the aforementioned publication may account for, or at least shed some light on, this phenomenon. A label heretofore unknown to me, referred to as "cool pose" espouses "a projection of toughness and aloofness, as well as other behaviors acquired in response to social pressures and slights. In the end, those behaviors can undermine academic performance and prevent black men from adjusting to campus life." According to this notion when responding to social pressures, black males often respond in this nonchalant and apparent unconcerned and unaffected manner as a means by which to project an imperturbable demeanor. From my own observation, this "toughness" was sometimes looked upon with great disdain by the African American females who were seemingly occupied with more serious agendas. Therefore it seems deeply-rooted discriminatory facets can be found within African American culture itself, directed not only towards the predominant white race, but towards divisional or even gender elements existing within its own community.

One additional component or possible built-in quasi-discriminatory element exists in the form of a practice commonly known as racial profiling. On the surface, "profiling" seems profoundly overt as a means in which to discriminate but, in truth, it may in some respects be an innate protective mechanism. Much in the same way that fear sometimes alerts us to avoid the possibility of danger, profiling, perhaps causes us to seek clues and advantage in challenging situations.

One evening late in the semester, I summoned my long time friend and acquaintance, Officer Scott Escobar, of the Buffalo Police Department, who as of late is assigned to that entity's motorcycle traffic division. For over twenty years, Officer Escobar, noted for his cool demeanor, (the type of cop who at the end of his shift places the badge, gun, and attitude in the top drawer) worked the 11:00 pm to 7:00 am shift, and by all accounts is well aware of the intricacies involved with being a white officer in a predominantly African American district. This particular evening, the officer's prescribed task was to lecture on aspects relating to the alleged practice of ethnic profiling as it relates to law enforcement. As his presentation began, I had the overwhelming sensation that I had just thrown him to the wolves, and as I exited the front of the room I proceeded to give him the proverbial thumbs up. Almost immediately he was assailed from all directions, with simultaneous shouts and assertions from students questioning as to why he and his department had stopped, had arrested or otherwise had harassed family and friends. After approximately sixty seconds of having epithets and indignities hurled at him, Officer Escobar shouted, "Hold up and listen to me people." "First and foremost," he continued, "I have a wife and two children," he explained, "and my primary objective at the end of my shift is to come home alive." This response now set the tone for further dialogue between officer and students. For approximately the next hour and a half, Officer Escobar politely and skillfully fielded questions giving insight and his own perspectives as a member of local law enforcement. The central theme of his argument seemed to center around the fact that if a car full of males was pulled over at 2:00 a.m. in the morning, irrespective of their race the Officer wanted those occupants of the vehicle either out on the ground or hands in positions where they could be judiciously and prudently monitored until backup could arrive, again all in an attempt to facilitate his primary task of returning home safely to his wife and young children. And, therefore, since the overwhelming complexion of America's inner cities is African American, what may at times appear as overt profiling is often disproportionately magnified or distorted due to programs implemented not out of malice but born rather of mere practicality. It would hardly be an accurate representation to suggest that the students warmly embraced all of his responses, but they gained a healthy respect or at the very least some insight as to the contentious and yet protective measures sometimes taken by the law enforcement community.

Afterwards, I went on to explain a similar situation, only in reverse, whereby my family and I too, were subject to police profiling. In August, 1970, my family and I departed for a trip down to Daytona Beach, Florida, driving a two door 1967 turquoise Chevelle, with blue and yellow New York State license plates. We descended south, traveling through Pennsylvania, Virginia and, after making our way through the Carolinas, we crossed the Georgia state border. As a boy of only 9, I was transfixed by the countryside and wonders to be seen abound. I most distinctly recall seeing what was formerly slave quarters still inhabited by African Americans, who now had in many instances luxury automobiles such as Cadillacs and Buicks parked on stone driveways, and with refrigerators and freezers on wooden front porches. The contrast to me was striking, and the immense poverty was everywhere. We had only just crossed the border when we were subject to a yelp, and resplendent flashing lights, which could be clearly seen in the rearview mirror. Immediately my mother glanced toward my father and inquired as to whether he had been speeding. "No more than five miles an hour," was my father's response. The predominant question at this moment was, "Why were we being pulled over?" My sister and I turned and glanced out the rear window in time to see a considerably overweight Georgia state trooper emerge from his vehicle, with an abundantly long radio antenna curled to the rear bumper and lights flashing. As the trooper made his way toward our vehicle he pulled his pants upwards over his large and rather protruding stomach, adjusted his hat and removed his large mirrored sunglasses. No doubt, he every bit looked the part, as he glanced down into the driver's window, (harshly and rapidly chewing gum) and demanded in a stern tone to see my father's license and registration. My father, acquiescing, provided the information, inquiring if there was a problem. "Shut your mouth, boy," was the response. After intensely studying the documents, he harshly returned them to my father, "Listen here, boy . . ." My father interrupted, "Who are you calling 'boy'?" My father did not intimidate easily, but my mother attempted to restrain him, "Larry please don't," she lamented. My father continued asking if it was necessary to frighten his wife and children for no apparent reason. The officer responded coolly, "I'm going to tell you once and only once, boy. You are going to turn this vehicle around and head back across into the South Carolina border, and if I ever see you here again, I will take you in. We don't need your kind around here." In the end he summed up the conversation with what appeared as a customary, "Ya'll have a nice day." As the trooper returned to his vehicle and restored his mirrored glasses to his face, my father growled, "It's the damn plates," and while glancing in the rearview mirror, my mother was in complete agreement. It wasn't the plates, as much as the more progressive views they represented. And, as such, were not welcome in what were then the last vestiges of the old South. I wasn't aware of it at the time, but apparently the phenomenon of racial profiling could make the transition from an ethnic one into an equally pronounced form of cultural profiling.

In the early 1980's when I was making my way through undergraduate school and studying criminal justice and pre-law and as a means to make my way through college, I sometimes took jobs in the related field of undercover security, primarily working for retail establishments in the area. The task at hand was to apprehend shoplifters so as to mitigate store losses. As a plain clothes detective I perused the store isles looking for potential shop lifters, ever aware that my job was contingent upon apprehending a set quota of the above-mentioned violators. As such, this was no easy task, since we had to, as a matter of store policy; maintain 100% visual observation of subjects and their movements. Even a momentary loss of observation might result in the subject dispensing with the stolen merchandise, and then a possible suit of false arrest or detainment might ensue. As a general rule, not one of malice, but rather of policy, I would often target either African Americans or people whose dress appeared disheveled and denoted probable lower class status. Since I generally worked the venues of suburban malls and establishments, these individuals often appeared out of sorts, and in fact were rather conspicuous. Moreover, the results tended to warrant this practice, as these were the persons I most often charged with the crime of petty larceny. Again, this was not affected out of any racial predisposition or bias, but out of necessity as my job was contingent upon productivity.

A similar quasi-bias existed towards men in general, who as shoplifters were perceived as potentially (and often verified), more violent than women, who as a rule were almost never handcuffed when remanded under arrest or into custody. This perhaps discretionary practice soon too ended, as my partner one afternoon arrested a female who had stolen hundreds of dollars in merchandise from the Craftsmen tool section of a local Sears. Upon her detainment, she was not handcuffed, and was escorted downstairs to be further interrogated and processed, when she produced a Craftsmen utility knife and proceeded to slash and hack my partner, who then required medical attention. Needless to say, after that precipitous event, I discriminated against men and women equally when taking the protective measure of handcuffing suspects. In my estimation, "profiling" as a rule, whether effected by law enforcement or other perfunctory entities, may in fact be more of a matter of instinct, learned experiences, and of survival (or at least a condition of perceived survival) than of any intended, prescribed and premeditated racial, ethnic, or even gender bias.

CHAPTER XI

Leveling the Playing Field

NO ONE COMPONENT to relations among the two races remains as divisive as perhaps the actions and programs designed to level the playing field in social, economic and political spheres. Irrespective of one's particular point of view, it is generally acknowledged that to some extent the cards have been stacked against the African American race at large. From the point of their forced integration in 1865 to the present, African Americans have mostly found themselves in the most disadvantageous of situations. Whether or not whites accept this, blacks indeed, in and of their own accord, have come to believe "the game" has been "rigged" against them. The fact that white household incomes and assets, outpace those of black families by a ratio of nine to one tends to bear this out ("Changing America" n.d. p. 33). Therefore, it should hardly be surprising that when and if African Americans are presented an opportunity in which to "even the score," they at times will seize it.

A most illustrative example of this theory can be found in the following; an acquaintance of mine who occasionally works in conjunction with the Niagara Frontier Transportation Authority, Western New York's mass transit system, indicated to me how that entity at times is compelled to deal with this peculiar aspect. On one particular afternoon police and fire units of the city of Buffalo were dispatched to a location near that city's waterfront and downtown area to respond to an accident with injuries pertaining to a Niagara Frontier Transportation Authority bus and a privately operated vehicle. My friend was among those units first summoned and upon arrival quickly assessed the situation to be less than critical. In fact, the bus, while attempting to make a rather wide turn, clipped a vehicle which was extended too far forward at an intersection. The impact estimated to be no more than probably ten miles per hour resulted only in minor physical damage to both vehicles in question; however, conditions on the bus itself were exceedingly more chaotic in nature. The overabundance of patrons on the bus were African American, many of whom were wailing and espousing injury especially to regions of the neck and back. My acquaintance, who has observed numerous injury accidents over the course of his career, could see no visible signs of injury, yet a plethora of those on board were packaged and removed by fire and E.M.S. units on backboards and Kendrix Extrication Devices, and then sent to local hospitals for assessment and evaluations. As it turns out, and as was explained to my E.M.S. acquaintance, the aforementioned authority has an unwritten policy whereby in order to circumvent accident litigation, claims involving those with documented clinical observation will generally be extended a small financial windfall, as a means to head off any possible future litigation. Moreover, it was further reported by my friend that two elderly white passengers were able to exit the bus of their own accord, both apparently unaffected and uninjured. To add insult to injury, those homeowners residing in the city of Buffalo and the surrounding community are required to pay a Niagara Frontier Transportation Authority transfer tax when buying, selling and or transferring real estate. This tax is designed as a means by which to subsidize a bus transit system that my family, I, and most of suburban Buffalo will never utilize. In truth, I have only ridden the system once after its completion, and then only as a matter of curiosity.

In a similar or related story, in 1995, buses of the N.F.T.A. became inextricably linked with an occurrence that drew significant national media attention, especially when the law offices of the nationally renowned Johnny Cochran became involved. The case focused on an extremely large and popular shopping mall located east of the city of Buffalo, and situated in a predominately white suburban area. The case involved the death of 17-year-old African American Cynthia Wiggins. "Because the mall banned city buses on some routes from dropping passengers on its property, Ms. Wiggins had to cross a busy seven-lane highway" to get to her job in the food court. (Chen, D.W., 1999, para. 2) It was while getting to work that Ms. Wiggins was hit and crushed by a dump truck. African Americans accused the mall of "racist transportation practices," whereby the highway acted as a "moat" to keep out some city residents. After the $2.55 million settlement, the bus stop was soon moved to a point inside the mall property ("Johnnie L. Cochran Jr. takes case." 1996. para 4.)

Therefore, the courts have historically been viewed as the great leveler in African American historical circles and continue to be manipulated effectively as a means by which to "level" the field. Civil courts and labor boards across the nation are backlogged with lawsuits and claims of wrongful discharge, alleging dismissal at the hands of overt or sometimes subtle racial discriminatory practices. More recently this has manifested under the guise of what is now commonly referred to as the "race card" and has become a fundamental component to all matters of discord between the races. My own wife, who in the world of business with over fifteen years of managerial experience has crossed this bridge more than once, when a black individual has their productivity, work ethic, or related behavioral patterns addressed by those in management, the race card is more often played than not. The supposition being, that the minority in question would not have been addressed, had it not been for their racial orientation. Often this results in African Americans and other minorities being permitted to backslide in order for management to circumvent, or to head off possible wrongful discharge actions, thus fostering further resentment among the predominant white class, who believe they are unjustly held to a higher standard. In my own dealings as a teacher, instructor or professor when issuing grades to minority students, I have often felt the necessity to insure that all my "I's" were dotted and "T's" were crossed before affixing them to paper. Unfortunately, it is precisely the above mentioned element which demands prudence and sensitivity when dealing with minorities in any capacity, in an effort to thwart any ramifications (legal, civil, or otherwise) in what might be the most litigious society in the annals of western civilization.

In an attempt to further level the fields and to assuage the races, programs centered around the concept of affirmative action have emerged as perhaps the most heinous and flagrantly inflammatory among the races. While addressing this topic in lectures it was often my observation that black students were more passive in their responses as a collective body, whereas the white students could barely contain themselves, at times even wriggling in their seats as though preparing to pounce at any moment. In a recent U.S. Supreme Court decision which both upheld and reaffirmed affirmative action programs in universities, Justice Sandra Day O'Connor's majority opinion emphasized the overall benefit to the majority of protecting diversity and stated that she "expects that 25 years from now" these programs may no longer be needed (Isaacson, Walter (2004) para. 3).

For more than two generations now these programs have been implemented in an attempt to level the playing field, as admittedly the white majority has run the business, political, and economic affairs of the nation at large. Since significant segments of the white culture harbors some degree of racism, so the theory goes, these attitudes and mores will ultimately manifest and transcend into all aspects of American culture from education to housing, and from employment to political equality. Therefore, an external force is requisite so as to impose some semblance to overall fairness or perceived equity. The task too large in scope to be dealt with on local or state levels, has been absorbed into the duties of the Federal Government and has emerged in the form and practices of affirmative action. To my white students, this is paramount to nothing short of discrimination in reverse and its legacy is every bit as abrasive today as upon its initial inception. The underlying element being that those equally qualified candidates whom are either white or whose credentials perhaps exceed those of the minority classes, will be passed over, and often with great regularity, in order that the respective playing field will be leveled. It is my assertion that next to the issue of welfare, this topic is the most antagonistic to whites (particularly in hard economic times), and the one which many believe to be most in need of redress.

I myself have been subject to this element of discrimination in reverse on more than one occasion. Having an educational background and degrees in criminal justice and pre-law, I have at numerous times attempted to pursue a career in law enforcement to no avail. On one particular instance, the city of Buffalo offered a civil service police exam, followed by a personal interview. As a prerequisite for the exam, it was further required that all candidates taking that exam at a local convention center be in possession of, at the very least, a two-year Associate's Degree. Upon my arrival to take the required exam, I found what must have been hundreds or even thousands of prospective candidates waiting in line to register for the exam, with the vast majority of those being African American. To me, it seemed hardly possibly that all of these candidates, in what appeared to be an endless line, could somehow be in possession of a college degree. After taking the exam, results were long in coming, far exceeding the advertised posting date. It was later revealed that the exam and its collegiate requirement were challenged as being discriminatory. Needless to say, I was never further contacted. Irrespective of the results and regardless of my educational credentials, I never truly anticipated being selected since I neither resided in the city, nor am I a minority.

In a related matter, a number of my colleagues assigned to my fire station, and those throughout my own department, routinely took the required civil service examination for the city of Buffalo. They too, all in possession of New York State Fire Fighting essential certification, many also holding Emergency Medical training cards and some even possessing college credentials were circumvented from the process, again largely attributed to residing outside of the city and their ethnicity. Not to my knowledge, did one of my colleagues ever secure an appointment to any of the aforementioned city emergency entities, as they too had possibly become victims of discrimination, but only in reverse.

Another particular aspect in which many of my students could identify with was those policies related to the skewing of intelligence or college entrance exams. It is general knowledge that many of our nation's prestigious universities or institutes of higher learning practice this policy as a means to attract minorities (many of those being African American) in an attempt to maintain some semblance of diversity (Nieli, 2010).

It has been further determined in sociological circles that many of these tests are often reflective more of white-oriented societal and educational experiences and therefore places minorities in disadvantageous situations when taking those tests or exams. Therefore, to level the playing field, those scores are adjusted accordingly or skewed by the adding of points based on the principle of minority labeling. There may, however, be some basis for this "disadvantageous situation" when placed under the microscope of scrutiny. For example, questions relative to technology such as computers, tends to favor the majority race as they are most often found in their own homes. In black homes where these perfunctory elements of technology are found to be lacking, they therefore could not be reasonably expected to respond well to questions about them. (Lefton & Valvutre, 1983, p. 327-332). Similarly, blacks too could not be reasonably anticipated to score favorably on issues relating to culture, theatre, or literature as once again their environments often do not harbor an abundance of these components. To attempt to reconfigure these tests would be an undertaking of mammoth proportions. To attempt to make them more equitable or at least reflective of minority's cultures who often take them would mean their composition would be subjective by nature, and again we would probably arrive back at square one.

To suggest that white culture holds the practices of affirmative action or skewed testing in great distain does not do the objective complaint justice. For family, colleagues and students of the white race, these discriminatory practices in reverse are nearly intolerable and abrasive. They are perceived as mechanisms designed not to level the playing field, but rather to place minorities in a more advantageous position, further enabling the minorities either to backslide or to strive for mediocrity, while whites are exponentially placed to higher standards. Again, blacks embrace these practices a necessary evil and make no apology for their continued existence. It appeared to me that the minority students in my classroom were either devoid of compassion towards this perceived discrimination in reverse, or either had become numb to its practice, or perhaps have even relegated it to the status of belated justice. As for my own point of view, I cannot say whether I support these practices, or whether I too, hold them in great distain, as they perhaps remain a necessary evil as again matters of the heart cannot be legislated. Nevertheless, their continued practices both foment and perpetuate hostilities, and further foster discord among the races.

Nonetheless, irrespective of whether one speaks about the United Negro College Fund, other associated programs, or the N.A.A.C.P.[2]), programs of this magnitude tend to emerge as equally divisive, rather than as mutually beneficial to the two races (Franklin & Moss, 2000, p. 353). When I reiterated that Du Bois' Niagara Movement was the predecessor to the more contemporary N.A.A.C.P., even I was shocked as to the contentious nature of the discussions in the classroom. To white students, the movement and subsequent organization represented something only slightly less than a

---

[2] The N.A.A.C.P.'S origins were deeply rooted in the Niagara Movement. Its organization was initially designed to raise awareness and to seek redress through the nation's court systems. Its inception in truth was an amalgamation of the more affluent elements of both races.

progressive black movement, which appears to metamorphose into an entity whose sole purpose seems, bent on the dismemberment of white values and culture. In short, it appears as equally offensive to white students as would a similar organization referred to as, say, the (NAAW) National Alliance for the Advancement of "Whitee" might appear to persons of color. Black students however, generally perceive the above-mentioned organizations only as a means by which to implement some measure of rectitude or to level the playing field in a largely otherwise white-controlled game, with some even suggesting that it nonetheless remains a necessary evil, again with the emphasis being placed on the word "necessary."

In a similar vein and perhaps equally offensive to the vast majority of white students, is the existence of the United Negro College Fund. Advertising for this organization solicits, in a "James Earl Jones" narrative voice, for donations for that particular fund, suggesting that "a mind is a terrible thing to waste." Again black students viewed this as a means by which to level the playing field. White students conversely and on the whole were adamant in their objection to this and any other such entity, citing that it is, in fact, black students who secure the overwhelming preponderance of student financial aid packages, primarily in the form of state and federal grants. The most heated of discussions ensued, with white students reminding their black counterparts that largely they, as "whites," were exempt from receiving anywhere near the amount of college dollars, as opposed to blacks whom they suggested were largely given aid, and a "free college ride." The resentment was most palpable. Moreover, white students, they continued, were often saddled with student loans sometimes to be repaid in what seemed for many to be perpetuity, while blacks who because of their alleged disadvantageous economic situation were required to pay little if anything in return. In a related matter, I interjected that my wife and I who already pay exorbitantly high taxes are forced to pay our own children's college costs due in part to our income level, and yet we are simultaneously expected to finance the education grants of low income recipients, including a fair amount of African Americans. A response to this comment, however, was never advanced by any of the collective student body.

Of all the multi-facets of America's contentious and fluid racial problems, few approach in breath and scope the magnitude of our welfare and social services network. An enormously disproportionate amount of America's tax dollars are diverted to sustain an overburdened and simultaneously abused system, whose initial conception was designed as a stop gap measure, but whose legacy is that of a permanent fixture, eroding the foundations of our nation's economic and social infrastructure and enabling successive generations to stay on the path of learned helplessness. Oddly enough, on the threshold of the Great Depression of the 1930's, it was the city of Buffalo's mayor who was among those leading the most clamorous objection to programs bearing a striking resemblance to wholesale welfare, which he believed in the end would leave a legacy of permanence rather than one of temporary governmental stewardship. In my own county of residence, the proportion of our county tax levy approaches nearly that of 80% of the tax base necessary to sustain those institutions. As fodder for classroom discussion, I could find little ground for commonality, as students on either end of the spectrum held firm to their points of view and convictions on this highly contentious topic. Their perspectives were most definitively manifested along racial lines. In my own estimation, poverty remains a close relative to the forces of racism, and nowhere is this better reflected than in the striking contrast between America's urban centers, which I have already described as bastions of poverty and deprivation, and the more affluent and pervasively white suburban areas. As for the vast majority of my minority students they represented the manifestation of those forces, as racism and poverty have long since been inherent fixtures of inner city communities. The pattern is repeated all across America from Buffalo to Baltimore and from Rochester to Richmond, the contrast is nothing short of embarrassing. These former industrial and cosmopolitan enclaves are no longer found to be bustling centers of commerce, but have become the nucleus of subsidization, whose mass transit systems and residents are sustained by the more affluent tax dollars surrounding them. White resentment to the programs of subsidization is both palpable and crescent, when programs such as food stamps, welfare and Section Eight housing, are paired with those of affirmative action and other associated programs designed to promote equality among the races.

In watching both races in my classroom debate this abhorrent topic wrapped in controversy, neither seems to be able to appreciate the other's point of view. Black forces in my lecture vehemently objected to being referred to as wards of welfare. They were adamant in their assertion that these programs were necessary to restore and maintain some semblance of parity with their more affluent white counterparts, who even at the present continue to marshal, command and control much of the nation's political and economic resources. The white minority in my class, however, remained obstinate in their adherence to the principle that an extraordinary and disproportionate degree of their tax dollars and income were being diverted to sustain a culture that was neither appreciative nor deserving of anything approaching the current levels. One comment advanced by a white student suggested that blacks (especially those residing in the city) never had it so good as recipients of "free rent, free school, and a free ride." Admittedly in the past, I myself have at times offered immense and vociferous objection to the fact that my wife and I pay an exorbitantly high proportion of our net income to help support numerous programs and classes including African Americans. The fact remains, however, that the white community is in possession of the lion's share of the nation's wealth, power and resources. Unless forced or required, the more affluent enclave would probably neither willingly share its resources, nor would it restrict discriminatory practices. Therefore, again, an external force imposed from above vis-a-vis the Federal Government is probably requisite to maintain some degree, if not at least a façade, of social equivalence.

At the end of my evening lectures I would gather my books and belongings, make my way to my new car, and make the journey through the city and its concourse of decay towards my own suburban residence of bright lights, shopping malls and activity. Sometimes on that approximately twenty minute ride, I would reflect upon the homes and circumstances to which my African American students were then returning, at times feeling ashamed, and yet simultaneously glad for my own fortunate set of circumstances. To the individual who asserted that "blacks who live in the city never had it so good," I ask the following, "Why is it then that you do not live or choose to reside there yourself?"

EPILOGUE

AS I SET pen to paper momentous changes both of the social and political spectrum are unfolding in American society: for the first time in our nation's over 200 year history, we have elected a black president. This, in and of itself, denotes some degree of progress in the realm of race relations. But we ought to be cautious and not presuppose that based upon a presidential election, the matter can be resolved or laid to rest. In all probability, this remarkable event should be construed as no more than a milestone to a much larger and more progressive journey. Among members of my own race it has been advocated that the election of an African American Executive is validation of the fact that equality between the races has at least in part been achieved, and that the issue may be close to resolution. The day after the election of President Barack Obama, Parisians were giving their commentary on the sweeping American election; one bank teller asserted "It's a sort of pardon of America for its slave past" (AP Article, 2008, November 4). Another suggested that finally America could put matters of race behind itself.

The problem I fear, however, is much more deeply-rooted. Electing a black president will only place a varnish on a problem which is significantly deeper and will not of its own accord assuage the anger of generations of African Americans who believe, and to some extent rightfully so, that they have been the recipients of the most egregious of injustices. Since the recent election of our forty-fourth president, two members of my own family, both members of management, have been forced to deal with issues of racial divide within their respective work places, and within the private sector. One instance resulted in the termination of a white female who sadly but adamantly and openly expressed her great hope that someone would eradicate the new President Elect. Through corporate intervention and subsequent teleconferences the woman was then suspended post haste. The second incident involved an African American woman, and occurred when a member of my family, also in management, was accused of having made racial comments in a cafeteria setting. That particular member of my family adamantly and explicitly denied any and all such utterances, and in turn alleged these charges were only initiated because the woman in question had been addressed previously over issues relative to work performance. Once again, corporate intercession was solicited, and fortunately the matter was dispensed with after the African American woman recanted, stating she had perhaps exaggerated her account of what had actually transpired. However, even though the statement was retracted by the black female, management proceeded to affect changes so that the black woman in question and other African Americans were made to feel more appreciated. Management was likewise compelled to implement additional "sensitivity" measures. Again a Presidential election, in and of itself, cannot mitigate the hostility of a people who have suffered centuries of depredation and indignity, and who at this juncture continue to seek political and social redress, as well as economic parity with their more affluent white counterparts.

The forced and abrupt integration of African Americans in 1865 into American society, and the subsequent manner in which it was conducted all but ensured that the road to racial equality would be a long and arduous one. An entire race was detached from its social moorings, in possession of few skills, utterly lacking in education, with no advance preparation, and was made to swim in the rapid currents of a predominantly white mainstream America. One of America's foremost Civil War historians, Bruce Catton, said it best when at the end of the great conflict he suggested, "Much work was left for later generations to do." "Perhaps," he continued, "the wonder is not that the job was done so imperfectly, but that it was done at all" (Flato, 1970, p. 209).

Therefore, racism does not occur in a vacuum and each and every racial slur and transgression only further delays our progress towards the ultimate destination of equality and social justice. Over the long-term, we have continued to pay the price for our mistakes of the past, and over the short-term we will probably continue to pay for them still, but progress is nonetheless possible. Nathan Bedford Forrest, the former Mississippi slave dealer and self made man who went on to become the legendary Civil War General, and later the first grand imperial wizard of the infamous Ku Klux Klan, provides us with a primary illustration and some cause for cautious optimism. Forrest, whom General William Tecumseh Sherman called, "the very devil himself," was known during most of his early and middle age years for his great disdain for blacks, and, as such, represented the social and moral values of much of the white South in the post Civil War era (Flato, 1970, p. 170). Nathan Forrest was a bit of a folk hero and was credited with the murder in April of 1864 of most of the black Union soldiers who had surrendered to his command at Fort Pillow on the Mississippi river. What happened that day was regarded as perhaps the most heinous atrocity of the war, and was forever known after as the "Fort Pillow Massacre." (Of the 262 black federal soldiers garrisoning the fort, only 58 were marched away as prisoners.) Forrest made no apology for his egregious behavior and following the war, he spear-headed the "K.K.K." and other associated efforts in several Southern venues.

Interestingly, however, later on in his life the former Confederate General began to call for the amelioration of the races (Foote, 1974, p. 110-112). Now, it is not known for certain what precipitated the mollifying of Forrest's position, whether later in life he was concerned with being compelled with each drawing breath, to be made accountable for past deeds, or whether it was achieved through a sincere change of conviction, but it appears that time may be the great imperative factor in matters of the heart. In many ways, this is reminiscent to me of the philosophy of a dear friend and former colleague of mine, who survived the horrors of a German labor camp during World War II, and who recently lost her officer son (a U.S. Military Captain) in Iraq. While teaching in Central Europe and after having just visited the Auschwitz concentration camp with her, I inquired with the utmost sincerity how she could emerge from the boughs of the most overt ethnic and racial discrimination of the twentieth century, with perhaps the most cheerful demeanor I have personally ever observed. She reminded me that sometimes as a matter of choice we have to choose to forgive, letting go of the latent hostility, blame and resentment lest it become all-consuming, pervasive and ultimately lead to our own destruction.

Equality among the races may prove to be too lofty a goal for our generation, but according to Bruce Catton, we may "at least" be "put on the road to completion" (Flato, 1970, p. 209). Matters of the conscience and of the heart cannot be legislated or mandated by programs such as affirmative action, or through Congressional statutes requiring civil rights enforcement or adherence. While I support the latter, programs of the former often prove to be counter-productive only furthering residual hostility and racial prejudices. Unfortunately, however, to some extent they have emerged as a necessary evil given that the nation's economic engines and social and political infrastructures remain in the control of the more affluent white culture. Therefore, as such the predominant white culture can reasonably anticipate that if the playing field is not "leveled" then blacks will continue to seek leverage or advantage, whenever or wherever opportunity presents itself, and that includes matters of subsidization, jurisprudence, and the more prevalent use of the "race card," all measures deemed as relevant to ensure that the playing field becomes more level or skewed in their direction.

In my own estimation, a more prudent and amenable approach would be to acknowledge African American contributions made to this country, not by means of restitution or legislative redress, all of which would only further agitate the white race (who already believe that through policies of affirmative action or governmental programs of welfare they have already paid more than their share for any transgressions of the past), but to promote the cause for the construction of a National Memorial in our nation's capital, by which to acknowledge the significant contributions made by all previous generations of African Americans towards the advancement of this country and its espoused and documented principles. A sculpture perhaps, not only of Dr. Martin Luther King, but one of sustenance and girth depicting scenes from the trans-Atlantic passage, slaves toiling in the fields, African Americans in arms, and ultimately those more illustrative of the civil rights movement itself. This I believe, would be more amenable to the races, and would propel us further on down the road towards the ultimate destination of justice and equivalence. Perhaps John Griffin put it most succinctly in his epic <u>Black Like Me</u>, when he suggested, "the real story is the universal one of men who destroyed the souls and bodies of other men (and in the process destroy themselves)," and, ". . . the story of the persecuted, the defrauded, the feared and detested" (Griffin, 1961). For over 300-years the matter of race in America has been one of sluggish but sustained progress, but one all too frequently plagued with moments of historical retrogression. Recounting in some degree the words of a Catholic priest, equality may not be the ultimate goal, but justice perhaps may be a more realistic, and a more attainable one, providing us with the best prospect for success. Irrespective, the two races have emerged as two divergent cultures, each bringing centuries of different ethnic, historical, and cultural experiences to the table, and who, collectively, despite a general lack of commonality and obstacles of intercontinental diversity, have conspired to propel and to advance the promise of a new nation.

As was generally the case, and in accordance with past precedence, the last lecture was reserved for my final summation and closing thoughts. When the class was solicited for any final opinions or comments a young black student (formerly of Rutger's) seated in a middle seat in the elevated back row immediately raised his hand, and in a somber and slow but deliberate manner rose and stated the following, "Mr. Weston," he said, "I would like to offer you an apology." I inquired as to why he was compelled to apologize. His response was shocking and simultaneously revealing. "After the first lecture," he said, "I returned home that evening and while dining with my family I informed them of my immense displeasure with having a white professor teach me African American history, and I expressed my intention to drop the course altogether." He continued by stating that "it was on his family's advice" that he continue on with the course in order to see whether I had something to offer to further his education on the subject. Moreover, he went on to indicate that he wished to profoundly apologize in that he did indeed learn from a white professor and that perhaps we might all learn something. In addition, he continued, he was ashamed at his own behavior, which he believed was tantamount to discrimination in reverse. I could hardly have been more surprised and pleased. His comments were followed by a general applause which was apparently the consensus of the balance of the class. It was at this juncture, listening to the spontaneous and sincere applause in which another revelation unfolded before me. As I glanced looking outward at the student body my eyes scanning left and right I discerned that the students were dispersed throughout the lecture room in an apparent random order, and in no way reflective of racial lines. To this very day I do not know whether this was affected through premeditated design or on some unconscious level. Irrespective of whatever the catalyst was, it was probably made possible by a conscious attempt at least in part to be receptive or understanding of another point of view and to educate oneself to perspectives other than one's own. This in no way is meant to suggest that the students wished to hold me in a warm and sustained embrace, or that we would sing "kumbaya" in unison, but rather that they understood from my own openness, and willingness to examine the African American experience, that a mutual comprehension was therefore possible and so too was progress. It would seem that an open heart and knowledge can tear down generations of mistrust, division and misconception. Ultimately it was I, the professor, who similarly was educated–not by textbooks or degrees but by the student body and the indomitable human spirit which, in the end, always prevails. Not all things, it turns out, can be gleaned from books alone, experience tends to be the great leveler.

Finally, in an unusual and remarkable turn of events, the Middle aged African American woman mentioned previously, and who displayed the most chagrin and outspoken objection to both my motorcycle, and to my presence in the classroom, was compelled several weeks after the conclusion of the semester to contact me in person, inquiring as to whether she could possibly utilize me as a future job reference. My response? That should already be apparent, if not return to page one of this text.

REFERENCES AND SOURCES

Ambrose, S. (1996). *Undaunted courage.* New York, NY: Simon & Schuster.

The American Experience. (n.d.). Retrieved from, http://www.pbs. org/wgbh/amex/fight/peopleevents/e_fights.htm

AP Article, (November 4, 2008).

Barry, R. H. (1901). *The true story of the assassination of President McKinley at Buffalo.* Robert Allan Reid Publisher.

Brown, R. C. & Watson, B. (1981). *Buffalo lake city in Niagara land*, Windsor Publications, Inc.

Changing America: Indicators of Social and Economic Well-Being by Race and Hispanic Origin (n.d.) retrieved from http://www.gpoaccess. gov/eop/ca/pdfs/ch5.pdf

Chen, D.W. (1999, November 18) Suit accusing shopping mall of racism over bus policy settled. *The New York Times.* Retrieved from http://www.nytimes.com/1999/11/18/nyregion/suit-accusing-shopping-mall-of-racism-over-bus-policy-settled.html)

The Chronicle Review, (2008). The Chronicle of Higher Education, Inc.

Clarkson, Thomas, M. A., (1836). *Cabinet of freedom*, (Vol. III) Published by John S. Taylor.

Colorado State University. (n.d.) Malcolm X–An Islamic Perspective, Retrieved from http://www.colostate.edu/Orgs/MSA/find_more/m_x.html,

Cox, C. (1991). *Undying glory: The story of the Massachusetts 54th regiment.* New York, NY: Scholastic.

Edgerton, R. B. (2001). *Hidden heroism, black soldiers in America's wars.* West View Press

Foote, S. (1974). *The civil war: A narrative.* (1st ed. Vol. 3) New York, NY: Random House

Flato, C. Narrative by Catton, B. (1970). The *Civil War.* American Heritage.

Franklin, J. H. & Moss, Jr., A. (2000). *From slavery to freedom a history of African Americans* (8th Ed.). McGraw-Hill.

Gandy dancer. (n.d.). In *Wikipedia.* Retrieved from, http://en.wikipedia.org/wiki/Gandy_dancer

Griffin, J. H. (1961). *Black Like Me.* New Jersey Library.

Higham, J. (1963). *Strangers in the land: Patterns of American nativism, 1860-1925.* New York, NY: Athenaeum.

Interactive Eli Whitney Biography. (n.d.). Retrieved from http://www.geocities.com/beberius/bio/WHITNEY/eliwhitney.html

Isaacson, Walter. (2004, April 26) Sandra Day O'Connor. *Time.* Retrieved from http://www.time.com/time/magazine/article/0,9171,994023,00.html

Jessie Owens, (n.d.) In *Wikipedia*, Retrieved from, http://en.wikipedia.org/wiki/Jessie_Owens

Joe Louis, (n.d.) In *Wikipedia*, Retrieved from, http://en.wikipedia.org/wiki/Joe_Louis

Lefton, L. & Valvatne, L. (1983). *Mastering psychology*. Boston, MA: Allyn & Bacon.

McKay, J., Hill, B. & Buckler, J. (1996). *A history of world societies*. (4th Ed., Vol B.) New York, NY: Houghton-Mifflin.

McKenna, D. (2009, January 16) The 3 to 5 million man march crowd estimates could lead to post-swearing-in swearing, history shows, *Washington City Paper*, Retrieved from http://www.washingtoncitypaper.com/articles/36682/the-3-to-5-million-man-march

Nieli, Russell K., (2010, July 12) How diversity punishes Asians, poor whites and lots of others, retrieved from http://www.mindingthecampus.com/originals/2010/07/how_diversity_punishes_asians.html

Norton, M. B., Katzman, D. M., Escott, P.D., & Chudacoff, H. (1998). *A people and a nation: A history of the United States*. (5th Edition, Vol. 1). New York, NY: Houghton-Mifflin

Norton, M.B., Katzman, M., Blight, D., Chudacoff, H., Paterson, T., Tuttle, W., & Escott, P. (2001). *A people and a nation*. (6th Edition, Vol. 1). New York, NY: Houghton-Mifflin

Norton, M.B., Katzman, M., Blight, D., Chudacoff, H., Paterson, T., Tuttle, W., & Escott, P. (2001). *A people and a nation*. (6th Edition, Vol. 2). New York, NY: Houghton-Mifflin

MuCollough, D. (2005). *1776*. New York, NY: Simon & Schuster.

Phillips, W. H. (n.d.) *Cotton gin*. Retrieved from http://eh.net/encyclopedia/article/phillips.cottongin

Reed, R. (1961). <u>The true story of the assassination of President McKinley at Buffalo</u>. Buffalo, NY: Buffalo City News

Staff Article. (1996, August 19) Johnnie L. Cochran Jr. takes case of black teen killed by dump truck on her way to mall. *Jet.* Retrieved from http://findarticles.com/p/articles/mi_m1355/ is_n14_v90/ ai_18610940/

U.S. Census Bureau, (2010). *Median and average square feet of floor area in new single-family houses completed by location* chart, retrieved from http://www.census.gov/const/C25Ann/sftotalmedavgsqft.pdf

---

Warren's common school geography, Cowperthwait and Co. 1866.

<u>Washington, Booker T. (1901). *Up From slavery.* The Riverside </u>Press.

www.ingramcontent.com/pod-product-compliance
Lightning Source LLC
Chambersburg PA
CBHW020303290526
45784CB00003B/1343